Who do you think you are?

Alice Harman

Blok Magnaye

Who do you think you are?

Find out about yourself
in 20 psychology tests

Contents

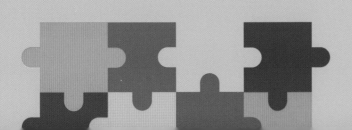

Websites, magazines, social media—they're all bursting with personality quizzes…**Which Disney character are you? What does your favorite cheese say about you? Which Hogwarts house do you belong to?** They can be a lot of fun (especially if you get a flattering answer), but is there anything more to them? What is the science behind personality tests—and what can you learn about yourself from taking them?

In **Who do you think you are?** we delve a little deeper into the many studies of self, picking apart fact from fiction to reveal the real you. You'll discover what personality is, and how all sorts of people have tried to measure and analyze it over the years. From ancient Greek scholars to modern psychologists that is, scientists who study behavior and the mind. Spoiler alert: there are a few odd ideas in the mix…

Try the twenty personality tests in this book, and discover what your results say about you. You'll learn all about the ideas and science behind the tests, too, so you can decide how seriously you want to take each one. Find out the difference between your personality type and your personality traits, uncover the truth behind the left brain–right brain myth, and dive deep into your mind to figure out where your special strengths lie. Are you a whiz with words, a marvel at math, or an ingenious inventor? And what sort of job might suit your interests, skills, and overall character best?

You'll discover how your personality can shape your life and the decisions you make—and how knowing a little more about yourself can help you find what makes you happiest.

But you'll also learn that, whatever your personality might be, it doesn't mean that you're stuck living your life in one particular way. Understanding your personality can help you think more clearly about the choices you make and the actions you take—and what feels right for you, no matter what anyone else thinks.

So, are you a thinker or a doer? Caring or cutthroat? Logical and orderly, or a creative free spirit who lives to dream? This book will give you a better idea about all that. But what you will also discover is that you are unique—just as we all are—and that's what makes life on Earth so complicated and fascinating.

Are you ready to get started? Then let's get quizzing!

What Is Personality?

Understanding personality

Before we start to measure our personality, we need to think about what it is that we're measuring!

So, what exactly is personality? In the most basic sense, we could describe it as what someone "is like." If we dig a bit deeper, we might think of personality as what makes us all see and interact with the world in different ways. Let's think about a real-life example…

Hanna and Carmen are best friends, and they're going to a party where they only really know the friend who invited them. Hanna is really excited about having a fun night and meeting new people. Carmen, on the other hand, really doesn't want to talk to lots of new people, and wishes she could stay at home.

At the party, Hanna walks straight up to a group of strangers, introduces herself, and starts joking around with them. Carmen hangs out on the edge of the group, listening rather than talking. Although Hanna and Carmen are in the same situation, they don't feel the same way about it and are behaving differently.

Getting to know you

So, does this example tell us what Hanna and Carmen "are like"? Not quite. Personality is all about patterns, so we can't learn all about it from just one party. But what if Hanna and Carmen tell us that this is pretty typical for them? It still wouldn't mean we understood their entire personalities, would it? Well, actually, some psychologists would say their behavior indicates their personality "type," which defines who they are.

But modern psychologists often prefer to think in terms of personality "traits"—patterns of thinking, feeling, and behaving that many of us share. For instance, in this example, Hanna might be described as outgoing and Carmen as more introverted, or maybe shy: neither trait is better than the other; they are just different. And one trait does not a personality make—to get an idea of what someone "is like," you'd have to learn about their other traits and how these traits interact with each other.

It is now widely believed that our personalities are incredibly complex, as unique as our fingerprints. You could share an identical set of traits with someone else and it still wouldn't mean you had the same personality. Your personality—the exact recipe for how your patterns of thinking, feeling, and behaving mesh together—is entirely your own.

Where does personality come from?

So how do we each come to have the personality that we do? Are we born with it, just like our fingerprints, or do we start out as a blank slate and develop a personality over time? And are we in control of forming our personality?

Scientists currently believe, based on studies of twins, that around 30–50% of our personality comes from our genes, and the rest is shaped by our environment. That means that your family and friends, and the things that have happened to you in your life, have played a part in making you the person you are today.

But you're not done yet. Research seems to suggest that until you reach adulthood, your personality can change a LOT. One apparent reason for this is a kind of "personality snowball effect": your personality influences the choices you make, and then the results of your choices influence your personality, and so on and so on, making certain parts of your personality stronger and stronger. And it's not all over once you become an adult, either. Although big, sudden changes in an adult's personality are much rarer, they can continue to change gradually over a lifetime.

Measuring Personality

Now that we know a little more about what personality is, how do we go about measuring it? And who does the measuring?

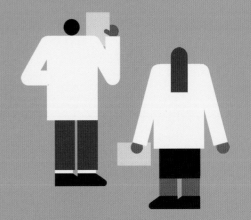

Who?

The second question is easier to answer, so let's start there. For official research purposes, it's usually psychologists. These are people who study psychology, the science of the human mind, and try to figure out why people behave the way they do.

But as we well know, anyone can make up a completely unscientific quiz—such as "What mythical creature are you most like?"—and invent their own measurement systems to judge someone's personality based on their answers. These tests are obviously meant to be fun, but the internet is also packed with more serious-looking tests made up by self-styled "experts" who actually have no scientific background at all—watch out for these, as they can give you all sorts of wrong ideas.

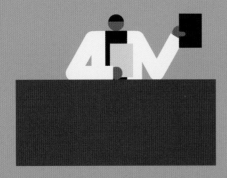

How?

The answer to this question is a bit longer and more complicated. Different psychologists and others in the scientific community—now and through history—have had all sorts of ideas about how to measure someone's personality. Some of them, as we'll see, are pretty weird and proven to be complete and utter nonsense (like, ahem, mapping the lumps and bumps on your head?), so let's put those aside for now and look at some of the more legit measuring tools available…

Talk time

For a long time, the main technique for measuring someone's personality was simply for an expert—a psychologist or something like one—to talk with them and analyze what they said. Have you ever heard of Sigmund Freud? Or Carl Jung? They were a BIG DEAL in the 20th century, and this was their whole thing. They, and many others, created their own complex system of ideas that they measured people against, based on what these subjects said—and how they said it. There are a few issues with this method: for one, it relies VERY heavily on the views of the person doing the testing; for another, there is no hard scientific evidence that either the "proof" being analyzed or the conclusions the analyst draws are actually correct.

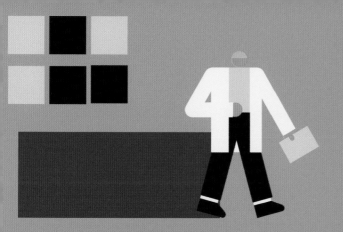
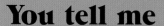
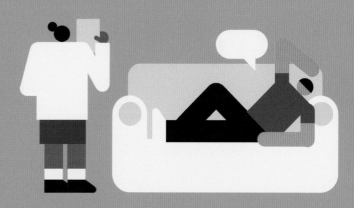

You tell me

In modern psychology, the main method of measuring personality is asking people to answer questions about themselves, often using questionnaires. The questions typically have set answers to choose from—such as yes or no, true or false, multiple-choice, or numbered-scale options—that give people a specific score. This score can be easily analyzed and compared with others' results, because everyone is being measured on the same scale. You'll get to know this measurement tool pretty well, because most of the quizzes in this book are based on it.

A bigger picture

Psychologists often use other tools alongside asking people to complete questionnaires about themselves. Why? Because sometimes the way we see ourselves can be a BIT different from how others see us—so it can be helpful to see someone from a few different angles. People's answers about themselves might be compared with what their family and friends, or strangers, say about them. Some researchers even get people to wear recording devices and compare how they speak and act to the answers they give in their questionnaires.

Brainiacs

As far as modern science is concerned, the human mind and the human brain are one and the same, so our personality exists inside our brain. Now that we can use brain-scanning machines to see the fascinating goings-on inside our skulls, researchers can learn more about how personality works. Our thoughts and feelings, and the behaviors that result from them, are processed as electrical messages zipping between the billions of neuron cells in our brain. Scientists can measure how this brain activity differs from person to person, and how it compares to what they—or others—say about their personalities.

A Brief History of Personality

Throughout human history, people around the world have tried to define different personality types and explain what makes each of us the way we are. Some of them sound quite strange now...

The four humors

The ancient Greeks believed that your personality was defined by the relative amounts of four liquids, called "humors," in your body. The idea was that too much of one humor made you behave in a certain way.

Too much **phlegm** makes you **phlegmatic**. In a word, you are **calm.**

Too much **black bile** makes you **melancholic**. In a word, you are **gloomy.**

Zodiac signs

Could your personality depend on something as simple as your birthday? That's the idea behind zodiac signs (also known as star signs), and it's one that has been around for thousands of years.

The twelve zodiac signs are sorted into four wider categories—earth, water, fire, and air—that each have their own associated personality traits.

If you're a Capricorn, Taurus, or Virgo, you are **Earth**. In a word, you are **practical.**

If you're a Cancer, Scorpio, or Pisces, you are **Water**. In a word, you are **emotional.**

If you're a Libra, Aquarius, or Gemini, you are **Air**. In a word, you are **curious.**

Too much **yellow bile** makes you **choleric**. In a word, you are **dominant.**

Phrenology

Want to know what someone is really like? Try feeling the bumps on their head…

It sounds pretty wacky, but around 200 years ago, this was considered the height of scientific personality testing. It is called phrenology, and it is…complete nonsense.

The idea was that different parts of the brain were responsible for different aspects of someone's personality. These parts grew when they were used, and shrank when they weren't, and the resulting bumps and hollows could be felt on the skull. In reality, though, these bumps have nothing to do with brain development at all.

Too much **blood** makes you **sanguine**. In a word, you are **fun.**

Pop psychology

Many websites and magazines today are full of personality quizzes, testing everything from "How good a friend am I?" to "What kind of pizza topping am I?"

Most people know this is just fun, but what if people in the future think we were actually serious? We might look like the strange ones…

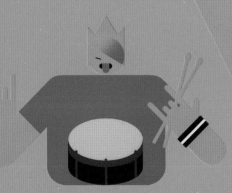

If you're an Aries, Leo, or Sagittarius you are **Fire**. In a word, you are **lively.**

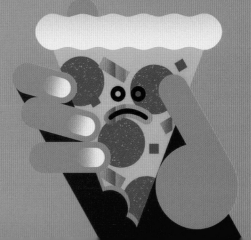

What's Your Humor?

Let's kick things off by finding out what the ancient Greeks would have made of you. Are you sanguine, melancholic, phlegmatic, or choleric?

1 If a friend came to you with a problem, what would you be most likely to say?

A "I know exactly what you need to do. Listen up..."

B "You know best, but I'm happy to talk through things for as long as you need."

C "Don't be sad. How about we get some ice cream to cheer you up?"

D "I'm so sorry you're feeling bad about this. Things are so hard sometimes."

2 What job would you most enjoy?

A Business owner

B Psychologist

C Actor

D Writer

3 Which Hogwarts house would you get sorted into?

A Slytherin, because I do whatever it takes to win.

B Hufflepuff, because I'm friendly and don't like drama.

C Gryffindor, because I throw myself into life.

D Ravenclaw, because I like to think before I act.

4 On a perfect Saturday evening, where would you be?

A Playing sports—and winning.

B At my best friend's house, watching a movie together.

C Out at a party, dancing and talking with everyone.

D Reading or drawing alone at home.

5 What do you think is your best quality?

A I stand up for myself and others.

B I'm a good listener.

C I'm fun to be around.

D I'm creative and think deeply about things.

6 And your worst?

A I lose my temper easily.

B I find it hard to stand up for myself.

C I'm pretty messy.

D I sometimes get too stuck in my own head.

7 When you work on a group project at school, what are you most likely to do?

A Take charge and make most of the decisions.

B Say that I'm happy to do whatever is most helpful.

C Make everyone laugh when things are getting boring or tense.

D Take on most of the work and not really talk to the rest of the group about it.

8 **What would you do on your dream vacation?**

A Camp in the mountains and explore the wilderness.

B Play board games with my family in a cozy countryside cottage.

C Hang out on a sunny beach all day with my friends.

D Spend lots of time reading or drawing, without anyone bothering me about it.

9 **In an argument with your best friend, what would you be most likely to say?**

A "I know I'm right, and I'm not giving in."

B "I don't want to argue. Let's work this out."

C "Haha, you look so angry. Come on, lighten up."

D Nothing, you would stay silent and walk away.

10 **You have loads of homework due tomorrow. What do you do?**

A Get on it as soon as I get home from school. It's a waste of time trying to avoid it.

B Relax for half an hour when I get home, then make a plan for what I need to do and work through it.

C Play video games at a friend's house until late in the evening, then rush to finish the work before bed.

D Sit staring at my books for a long time, worrying about doing a bad job, before eventually starting.

Mostly B = Phlegmatic

A phlegmatic person is loyal and consistent, an easy-going and gentle soul who is happier observing and listening than being the center of attention. They dislike conflict, and try to keep people happy and resolve issues peacefully.

Mostly C = Sanguine

A sanguine person is fun, optimistic, and excited about life. They love being around people and usually have lots of friends, but they tend to be impulsive and disorganized and can sometimes let people down.

Mostly D = Melancholic

A melancholic person is sensitive, idealistic, and creative, and often craves time alone to think deeply about the world. They can get stuck inside their head and come across as serious and moody, but they care enormously about getting things right.

Mostly A = Choleric

A choleric person is ambitious, knows their own mind, and doesn't let anything get in their way. They love a challenge and are confident and passionate, but their quick temper can cause problems with others.

Which Zodiac Sign Should You Be?

Now, let's look to the stars…Never mind your actual zodiac sign, at heart are you a Water, Earth, Air, or Fire personality?

1 You have to choose between taking two subjects at school. What is going through your head?

A "I need to think really carefully about this. I'll be so annoyed at myself if I choose the wrong one."

B "I know in my heart which one I want to pick, so I'll just go with that."

C "Either one will be fine. The important thing is that it's my own choice to make.'

D "Argh, I can't make up my mind. I wish I didn't have to choose."

2 If you have to stay inside on a rainy Saturday. How do you feel about it?

A Bored and grumpy.

B Great, it gives me a chance to organize all my things.

C So relaxed. I love staying in. I can lie around daydreaming for hours.

D If I've got a book or homework to focus on, fine. If not, I'm all fidgety and restless.

3 What do you like most about your best friend?

A I can trust them completely and be myself around them.

B They're really smart and interested in lots of different things.

C They understand me so well and really care about my feelings.

D They speak their mind and they're really fun to be around.

4 Your friends tease you for being a bit of a...

A Control freak.

B Show-off.

C Sensitive soul.

D Nerd.

5 What's your favorite kind of movie?

A Romantic dramas—even though they always make me cry.

B Smart, funny high-school comedies.

C Documentaries and movies based on real-life events.

D Fast-paced thrillers and action movies.

6 **How do you feel about school uniforms?**

A They can stop people feeling bad about not having expensive clothes, so I think they're a good idea.

B Ugh, I hate them. They make everyone look the same.

C I don't really like them. You should be free to express yourself through your clothes.

D I get the point of them, but I think it's okay to bend the rules by wearing something that isn't part of the strict uniform.

7 **Which animal do you feel the strongest connection to?**

A Dolphin.

B Owl.

C Lion.

D Bear.

8 **If your best friend was looking for you at a party, where would they know to find you?**

A Right in the middle of things, dancing and having a lot of fun.

B Deep in conversation with one or two people.

C Organizing a game for everyone to play.

D Hanging at the edge of a group of people, feeling a little bit awkward.

9 **What's your favorite season?**

A Spring.

B Summer.

C Autumn.

D Winter.

10 **Think back to the last time you apologized to a friend. What was the reason for it?**

A I said exactly what was on my mind, and it hurt their feelings.

B I hadn't realized that they wanted my help with something, and they'd felt neglected.

C I didn't listen to them, and they felt like I'd bossed them around.

D I knew that someone was spreading rumors about them, but I didn't tell them because I didn't want them to get upset.

Answers on page 18

Answers

Are you ruled by Earth, Fire, Water, or Air? To find out, count up how many of your answers fit with each type.

1. **A** Earth
   B Water
   C Fire
   D Air

2. **A** Fire
   B Earth
   C Water
   D Air

3. **A** Earth
   B Air
   C Water
   D Fire

4. **A** Earth
   B Fire
   C Water
   D Air

5. **A** Water
   B Earth
   C Air
   D Fire

6. **A** Air
   B Fire
   C Water
   D Earth

7. **A** Water
   B Air
   C Fire
   D Earth

8. **A** Fire
   B Air
   C Earth
   D Water

9. **A** Fire
   B Water
   C Air
   D Earth

10. **A** Fire
    B Air
    C Earth
    D Water

Earth

Capricorn, Taurus, Virgo

You like to get things done, and you like to do them your way. You are organized, disciplined, and practical, and people can always count on you. You are a perfectionist and can find it hard to believe that anything you have done is good enough. You are a caring and loyal friend, but you can sometimes struggle to understand other people's points of view.

Air

Libra, Aquarius, Gemini

You're a "head over heart" person who looks at the world logically and loves learning new things. You can find it hard to make up your mind, which frustrates you because you like to get things done quickly. You can sometimes get lost in your thoughts, but you are great at telling stories and are a very interesting person to talk to.

Water

Cancer, Scorpio, Pisces

You feel all the feels, all the time. You care deeply about other people and the world, and it really upsets you when bad things happen. You are creative and imaginative, and you trust your instincts. You are a kind and loving friend, but you can be sensitive and sometimes worry that people don't like you.

Fire

Aries, Leo, Sagittarius

You're the life and soul of every party. A natural performer, you have lots of energy and charm and you love being the center of attention. You are very ambitious, and you say what's on your mind, which more sensitive types can find difficult. You like to do what you want, and don't like being told no.

What Kind of Meal Are You?

This isn't anything to do with your favorite foods, oh no! This is about peering inside your mind and seeing what kind of delicious dinner most reflects who you are...

1 **Which after-school sport would you rather join?**

A Soccer, because my friends do it and I like being part of a team.

B Do I have to? Ugh, fine—chess, because I can sit down while I do it.

C Just one? I want to do ALL the sports.

D Cross-country running—I like to be on the move.

2 **What kind of birthday party would you like best?**

A A celebration at home with family.

B A relaxed dinner with friends at a local restaurant.

C Doing an escape room or playing laser tag.

D I don't like a big fuss. I'd rather skip it altogether.

3 **What's the first thing you do when you wake up?**

A Snuggle further under the comforter and enjoy feeling cozy.

B Groan and hit the snooze button.

C Leap out of bed, ready to face the day.

D It depends—every day is different.

4 **What do you like to do while you're watching TV?**

A Make crafts, especially cards.

B Message my friends.

C Create bright patterns in a coloring book.

D Do my homework—I'm a great multitasker, honest.

Mostly A = Hearty stew
You are a warm hug of a person, who loves feeling cozy and spending time with others. You make people feel safe and cared for, especially if they're a bit down.

Mostly C = Salad
Colorful and fresh, bursting with energy, your positive attitude lifts people's spirits. You have a sunny, creative vibe and you enjoy challenging yourself to be the best.

5 How would your best friend describe you?

A Warm.

B Laid-back.

C Colorful.

D Busy.

6 It would most upset you if someone at school called you...

A Unkind.

B Uptight.

C Lazy.

D Arrogant.

7 What was your favorite toy when you were younger?

A My raggedy old teddy bear.

B Walkie-talkies—I had one, my friend next door had the other.

C Colorful building blocks.

D My tricycle.

8 What kind of music do you like best?

A Sweet, slow love songs.

B Cheesy pop I can sing along to with my friends.

C Upbeat electronic and hip-hop that I can dance to.

D All sorts—I couldn't pick just one kind.

9 If your parents won the lottery, what would you ask for?

A A pony—I'd take such good care of it.

B A massive party for me and all my friends.

C A beach vacation.

D A state-of-the-art road bicycle.

10 Which hat would you be most likely to wear?

A A wool beanie.

B A baseball cap.

C A straw sunhat.

D A bucket hat.

Mostly B = Pizza

You're sociable but laid-back, and you love nothing more than kicking back with your friends on the sofa. You don't try too hard, and everyone loves you for it.

Mostly D = Sandwich

Always on the move, you like to take advantage of everything life has to offer. You have a straightforward, open-minded approach and you don't like too much fuss.

Personality Types

We all like to think we're special—and we are. But some psychologists think that everyone's personality can also be defined as a certain "type," based on the different ways that we understand and interact with the world around us.

Carl Jung's personality types

Carl Jung was a very famous Swiss psychologist. His book *Psychological Types* was published nearly a century ago and still hugely influences the way we think about personality.

Jung thought that the most important, defining feature of someone's personality was whether they were an "extrovert" or an "introvert." So, what exactly does that mean? Read over the descriptions below and see which one you think fits you best…

I = Introverted: You tend to like spending time alone, and being around other people—especially big groups—really tires you out. You are quite sensitive, and sometimes you get overwhelmed by things and just want some peace and quiet.

E = Extroverted: Being around others gives you energy, and you tend to prefer doing things as part of a group. You get excited quite easily and you enjoy being out and about, feeling like you're taking an active part in the world.

Jung wasn't suggesting that we are all one of only two personality types, though. He believed that just as we all have either an "extrovert" or "introvert" attitude, we also have a preferred way of understanding the world: sensing, intuiting, feeling, or thinking.

S = Sensing: You pay close attention to the world and focus on facts, trying to see things as clearly and simply as possible.

N = Intuiting: You use facts as a starting point, and make sense of things by interpreting them and linking them together in your own way.

F = Feeling: When you make a decision, your top priority is the effect it will have on people—you want to make yourself and others happy, above all.

T = Thinking: You base your decisions on logic, and it's more important to you to be correct than to make yourself and others happy.

Jung presented these four options in two pairs, "Sensing or Intuiting" and "Feeling or Thinking." Although he believed we all do some of each, depending on the situation, each person tended to identify most closely with one trait from each pair. In total, Jung thought there were eight personality types.

Myers–Briggs Type Indicator

What's better than eight personality types? How about sixteen? The Myers–Briggs Type Indicator, based on Jung's ideas about personality types, is one of the most well-known and widely used personality tests in the world today.

Katharine Cook Briggs and her daughter Isabel Briggs Myers adapted Jung's ideas into a structured personality test that people could fill in themselves, rather than speaking to a psychologist. They added another category, "**Judging or Perceiving**," which focused on whether someone preferred things to be structured and fixed or open and flexible.

The results of their personality test come in the form of a four-letter code—for instance, ESFP is an Extrovert who favors Sensing, Feeling, and Perceiving. There is no "best" or "worst" type, but the organized, complex, and creative INFJ type is thought to be the rarest.

Insights Discovery

Another modern self-test based on Jung's ideas of personality types is Insights Discovery, which is particularly popular in the workplace. It defines four personality types, each linked to a different color—red, blue, green, and yellow.

The idea is that everyone has a mix of colors, but one dominant one, and that each color has its own strengths and potential weaknesses. In the workplace, it aims to give managers an idea of how their employees work best, relate to others, and like to be treated.

What Personality Type Are You?—Animals

In this quiz, as with the Myers–Briggs Type Indicator and other tests based on Jung's ideas about personality, the answers you give will result in a four-letter "code" representing your score in four character categories.

Answer the questions on pages 26–27, translate your answers into a code on page 30, then find the animal that matches your code here. Are you a loyal Bear? A free-spirited Otter? Or perhaps a crafty Crow...?

Octopus (ISTO): You love experimenting and figuring things out, and can turn a hand (or should that be a tentacle?) to most things.

Hummingbird (ISFO): You love zipping around, exploring new things, and charming people with your can-do attitude.

Wolf (ESTO): You like living on the edge, always alert to everything that is going on around you and quick-thinking enough to act on it.

Hyena (ESFO): It's never boring when you're around. You throw yourself into life and love to laugh and entertain others.

Elephant (ISTC): You never forget your responsibilities, and you are guided by solid facts rather than emotions and passing whims.

Bear (ISFC): You are fiercely loyal to those you love, warm and caring but also willing to step up to protect people.

Ant (ESTC): You are known for getting things done, organizing people and things to achieve impressive results.

Dog (ESFC): You are friendly, sociable and always ready to offer a helping hand—or paw. No wonder you're so popular.

Owl (INFC): You have a quiet wisdom beyond your years, which inspires others and helps you do good in the world.

Dolphin (INFO): You believe in helping people, and your caring attitude and love for life makes others happy to be around you.

Tiger (ENFC): Your confidence and charm make for a striking presence, and people find themselves wanting to listen to you.

Otter (ENFO): You are a fun-loving free spirit who loves getting creative and spending quality time with others.

Monkey (ENTO): You are endlessly curious about the world, and love a challenge that really tests your intelligence.

Lion (ENTC): You are a born leader, driven to use your confident, fearless attitude to make things happen.

Crow (INTO): You love learning and puzzles, using your intelligence creatively to come up with new inventions and solutions.

Squirrel (INTC): Smart and hardworking, you are always thinking ahead and putting plans into action that will pay off in time.

True or False?

Answer these true-or-false questions to discover your personality type—and the animal that best represents you.

Don't think too long before you give your answer, as the test works best when you go with your gut reaction. Remember, there are no wrong answers.

1 To remember dates in history class, I need to have a big-picture idea of what was happening at that time.

T or F

2 When I'm with my friends, I tend to listen more than I talk.

T or F

3 If my friend was really happy with their new haircut and asked me if I liked it, I would say yes even if didn't.

T or F

4 If I kept giving correct answers in class and another student called me a "robot," I'd be upset.

T or F

5 I like making revision plans and to-do lists for my schoolwork.

T or F

6 I get bored and restless when I spend time alone.

T or F

7 I don't like making plans with my friends for the weekend. I'd rather decide on the day what I feel like doing.

T or F

8 I would rather take a multiple-choice test than write an essay.

T or F

9 For a school project, I'd rather be paired with someone nice than someone who gets good grades.

T or F

10 Parties make me feel fired up and full of energy.

T or F

11 If two of my friends are arguing and I'm not sure exactly what happened, I still usually have an opinion about it.

T or F

12 I tend to avoid doing my homework until the last moment.

T or F

Answers on page 30

What Personality Type Are You?—Shapes

This quiz has nothing to do with what your favorite shape is—if you even have a favorite shape. Each shape stands for one of four personality types, which each relate to other people in very different ways.

1 **Which of these things would you be most likely to do, if no one would find out?**

A Cheat on a test to get the highest grade in the class.

B Listen in on a conversation to see if people were talking about me.

C Rearrange groups in class so I don't have to work with people who always take over or aren't very nice.

D Study by myself in the library rather than go to class so I don't have to put up with other students' stupid questions and behavior.

2 **When I finish school at the end of the day, on the way out I...**

A Run or walk as quickly as I can, and get annoyed if people are in my way, slowing me down.

B Find my friends, and chat with them for as long as possible before I have to go.

C Take my time walking out, saying hi to people as I go.

D Put my head down and my headphones in so I can get home without anyone bothering me.

3 **If you overheard friends talking about you, what would hurt you most to hear?**

A You're not as impressive as you think you are.

B You're not as popular as you think you are.

C You're not as nice as you think you are.

D You're not as smart as you think you are.

4 **If a new student started in your class at school, how would you feel?**

A Competitive—are they going to try to outdo me?

B Excited—I want to be the first one to talk to them.

C Protective—it's so hard being the new person. I'll make sure to smile and say hello.

D Uninterested—I don't get along with most people, unless we are very similar, so I'll ignore them.

5 **If you became a YouTube sensation overnight, how would you feel?**

A Finally. I'm going to make sure I stay at the top where I deserve to be.

B This is amazing. I love all my new fans. But the negative comments make me so sad…

C Wow, this is a lot of pressure. I hope I don't upset anyone by accident.

D Suspicious…do these people actually like me, or are they just making fun of me?

6 **If you were in a race and the person just ahead of you fell over, what would you do?**

A Secretly think, "Yes, one fewer person to beat," and speed right past them.

B Do a comedy fall next to them, to make everyone laugh, then help them up.

C Stop and help them, reassuring them it's all okay.

D Think about helping, but then decide it's not my place or problem and keep going past them.

7 **You're moving house, to a slightly bigger place a few roads over. How do you feel?**

A Great. I love change, as long as it's in the right direction—bigger and better.

B Sad to leave our current neighbors, but excited to meet all our new ones.

C Concerned that everyone seems quite stressed, but I'm putting a happy face on so no one worries about me.

D Annoyed. It's a stupid idea, the house is barely different and it's in the same area. What's the point of all this fuss for no reason?

8 **Your friend posts a photo of you on social media where you're making a weird face. How do you feel?**

A I'm furious. How dare they? It's pathetic that they're so envious of me that they have to try to destroy me like this.

B I'm really happy that everyone finds it so funny.

C I don't love it, and I would have asked them before posting a picture like that of them. But I'd rather let it go than confront them about it.

D I'm annoyed and embarrassed, but this is the sort of careless behavior I expect from most people.

9 **What would you do if your friend was telling a story to a big group about a time when you were there too, and they were exaggerating a LOT?**

A Call them out for making things up, and tell everyone what really happened.

B Join in laughing, and jump in with my own funny, exaggerated details.

C Laugh along with the others, and stick up for my friend if anyone suggests they're making it up.

D Walk away. I don't like big groups or show-offs, so this sounds like my worst nightmare.

10 **Which kind of TV show would you rather watch?**

A A tough reality-TV competition show.

B A laugh-out-loud comedy about a group of friends.

C A factual show about people working together in a school or a hospital.

D A challenging, long-running quiz show.

Answers on page 31

Answers

Ready to find out what personality type you are—and what animal and shape that makes you?

Quiz 1—Animals

To find out your four-letter personality type, simply add up how many of each letter your answers match up to. There are three questions relating to each of the four categories, so you should have a clear winning letter in each category.

The options in each category are:

Extrovert (E) or **Introvert** (I)   **Sensing** (S) or **Intuiting** (N)

Thinking (T) or **Feeling** (F)   **Controlled** (C) or **Open** (O)

Jung's personality types (explained in more detail on pages 22–23) only include the first three categories. The fourth category is focused on your attitude toward control—whether you prefer to leave things freer and more open, or you enjoy a more structured life. This is an area that many psychologists now think is also key to understanding our personality.

1.   True = N, False = S
2.   True = I, False = E
3.   True = F, False = T
4.   True = F, False = T
5.   True = C, False = O
6.   True = E, False = I
7.   True = O, False = C
8.   True = S, False = N
9.   True = F, False = T
10. True = E, False = I
11. True = N, False = S
12. True = O, False = C

So, what's your four-letter code?
Does it ring true with what you feel about yourself?

Now for the moment of truth...
Turn to pages 24–25 to discover which animal you are at heart.

Quiz 2—Shapes

Are you a sharp triangle, a smooth circle, a stand-out star or a no-nonsense square? Let's find out.

Mostly A = Triangle

A triangle personality knows what they want and really goes for it. They will fight their way to the top of the pile no matter what, turning everything into a competition, and it doesn't always win them friends. But many people respect them for speaking their mind and fighting to make their mark in the world.

Mostly C = Circle

A circle personality is a gentle soul who wants everyone to be happy and get along. They like things to be fair and equal, and they would rather work together with others than compete with them. They are afraid of seeming negative or arrogant, and are more comfortable looking out for others than standing up for themselves.

Mostly B = Star

A star personality is fun, loud, and loves being the center of attention. They are happiest in a big crowd and love making people laugh. They care a lot about what others think, and it can really upset them if they think someone—even a stranger—doesn't like them.

Mostly D = Square

A square personality likes things to be done in a certain way—the right way. They feel most comfortable with rules, order, and routine, and when people don't respect those things, it can really upset them. They can sometimes appear cold and critical, but you can always rely on them to be honest and do their best.

The Big Five Quiz

How do you think you measure up against each of the Big Five factors of personality: Openness, Conscientiousness, Extroversion, Agreeableness, and Neuroticism?

Give a score from 0 to 5 for each of the following statements—0 means you completely disagree with the statement, 5 means you absolutely agree with it. Make a note of your scores, in the right order.

1 I love telling stories or jokes to big groups of people, especially if everyone's attention is just on me.

2 If I see a sad commercial on TV—for example, one for a charity that helps animals who have been hurt and abandoned—it makes me feel really down and it takes ages before I stop thinking about it.

3 I love thinking up stories, and I find that new ones pop into my head really easily.

4 When I have a big test coming up at school, I don't really worry about it much and I find it a bit odd when people get super stressed about it.

5 I always do my chores around the house as soon as I'm asked, and I make sure to do them properly.

6 It makes me feel really sad when my friends are upset, and I want to do everything I possibly can to help them feel better.

7 When I'm in a group of friends or other people I know, I listen more than I talk.

8 I lose things all the time, and I find it really hard to keep things tidy and in the right place.

9 If I went to have dinner at a friend's house and their parents made something I'd never eaten before, I really wouldn't want to try it.

10 I'd find it really annoying if I wanted to go and do something fun and my friend was being all sad and mopey and kept talking about their problems.

Answers on page 36

Answers

So, how agreeable, conscientious, neurotic, extroverted, and open are you? Let's find out!

This quiz was secretly split up into questions that tested the different Big Five personality traits—two questions for each one. To find your overall score for each trait, you need to take away your score for the second question from the first one.

For example, questions 1 and 7 tested Extroversion. If you scored yourself 2 for question 1 and 5 for question 7, your overall score is -3.

Extroversion = questions 1 and 7
Neuroticism = questions 2 and 4
Openness = questions 3 and 9
Conscientiousness = questions 5 and 8
Agreeableness = questions 6 and 10

What are your scores for each trait? Are you surprised?

Your results

The most common score for each trait is somewhere in the middle, which in this quiz would be -1, 0, or 1. This means you're pretty balanced between the two extremes of that trait—for example, a score of 1 for Extroversion means you have introverted and extroverted tendencies and only lean ever so slightly toward being more extroverted.

Learn a bit more about what a low or high score means for each trait. If you have these scores, do you agree with what they apparently say about you?

Agreeableness

Low score (-5 to -2): You tend to look out for number one—yourself! You don't like compromising on what you want, and you don't really care how others feel as long as you get your way. A strong will can be very useful, but you may come across as unfriendly and rude—try thinking about others' feelings a bit more.

High score (2 to 5): You go out of your way to care for others and make life as easy and nice as possible for them, even if it goes against what you want. The world needs more considerate, trustworthy people like you, but be careful that more selfish personalities don't take advantage of your kindness.

Neuroticism

Low score (-5 to -2): You are very emotionally stable, which means that you don't tend to have massive mood swings or easily lose your temper. Obviously everyone feels sad, angry, and scared sometimes, but in general you are pretty calm and you usually bounce back quickly if you do experience difficult times.

High score (2 to 5): You are a sensitive person, and can often feel down, worried, or very angry. You care deeply about things and it feels like you can't help reacting strongly to them. Be careful to ask for help if things feel like they're getting too much—no one expects you to deal with everything alone.

Conscientiousness

Low score (-5 to -2): You have an easygoing, devil-may-care attitude to life and don't take yourself—or many other things—too seriously. You're not bothered about things being orderly or going to plan, but it's good to remember that some people do care about those things and you can upset or hurt them without even realising.

High score (2 to 5): You always have a plan and you like to stick to it! Many people really appreciate how reliable and organized you are, and being so on top of things is very helpful for success at school and in the workplace. However, it's also important to learn how to be flexible—and to take a break occasionally!

Extroversion

Low score (-5 to -2): You are pretty introverted, which means that you like having time to think over things and be alone rather than having to be "on" and chatty with people all the time. You can be reserved and quiet, but that doesn't mean you don't like socializing or don't want friends—it just tires you out!

High score (2 to 5): Hellooo, you're just bursting with extrovert energy, aren't you?! Party hosts probably love you as much as you love parties—you're fun, excitable, and a great conversationalist. Try to remember that some people can find your confidence a bit intimidating, though, and shier people often have lots to say if you give them a chance!

Openness

Low score (-5 to -2): You like to know exactly what's happening when, and changes to your routine can make you very uncomfortable. You can be just as cautious in how you think about things, unwilling to get too "out there" and try new things. Be careful not to close yourself off too much—or to judge others for doing things differently.

High score (2 to 5): Curious, creative, and imaginative, you want to try everything that life has to offer! People might sometimes think you're a bit wacky, but who wants to think and do things just like everyone else? You believe life is for exploring and adventuring—just remember that some others aren't quite as brave as you are, so be kind and give them time.

Plotting your results

Draw a copy of this graph and plot your scores for each trait. Connect up the plot points—does the line zigzag up and down a lot or do you have fairly similar scores across the five traits? Do you have one or two dominant traits, which have scores very close to the bottom or top of the graph?

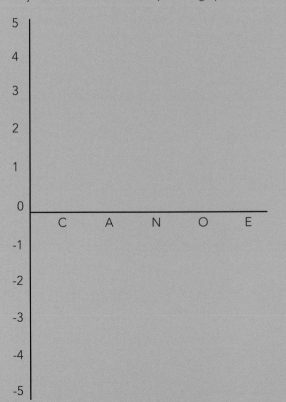

37

Left Brain

A quick search online throws up all sorts of quizzes and articles to help you figure out whether you're **"left-brained"** or **"right-brained"**—that is, which side of your brain has more influence over how you think, learn, and act.

The left side of the brain is thought to be logical and to love language, rules, and order. The right, however, is kind of the wild side—it is creative, impulsive, and makes decisions based on feelings rather than facts. So you might hear people describe themselves as right-brained if they like to think of themselves as freewheeling, artistic souls—or as left-brained if they believe they are logical, fact-driven, and good at working with data.

The only problem is…it's not true. Different parts of the brain are responsible for different things—for example, areas at the front of the brain are linked to smell and speech—but there isn't a simple left–right divide in ways of thinking.

The idea of having a "left-brained" or "right-brained" personality is very popular, but essentially a sort of urban myth—something that is widely believed but doesn't actually have any evidence to support it.

It's easy to see how people came to believe it, though—back in the 1800s, doctors noted that people who had suffered terrible injuries to certain parts of their brain could start behaving very differently. So far, so good…

Then, in the 1960s, Roger Sperry and Michael Gazzaniga carried out a number of experiments on people who had

Right Brain

undergone brain surgery in a dramatic attempt to stop them having epileptic fits. The surgery had involved cutting the corpus callosum, a thick band of nerve fibers between the two sides—the left and right hemispheres—of the brain.

This meant that the patients' brains were essentially split in two, and the separated brain hemispheres could no longer "talk" to each other.

In their experiments, Sperry and Gazzaniga found that the brains of these patients reacted differently in tests to how an intact brain does. This told them that the two sides of the brain carry out different processes. So far, still so good.

However, over time, people without expert knowledge of brain science have oversimplified these ideas about brain function. They and others have then made the leap to forming judgements about personality types based on this incorrect information.

The truth is, the human brain is incredibly complex and experts still don't fully understand how all the different parts of the brain work together to carry out the huge variety of processes of which it is capable. But what is absolutely clear is that the world isn't divided into two camps of left-brainers and right-brainers.

We're all whole-brainers.

Left Brain–
Right Brain Quiz

As we've seen, the whole idea of someone being "left-brained" or "right-brained" isn't quite right...

So this quiz is about whether you have more of the characteristics traditionally associated with being one or the other—for example, do you find it easier to learn and remember things by seeing them? Do you obey the rules, or want to break them? Discover how you think and learn—using your whole brain.

1 **If you're trying to learn how to do something, such as beat a tricky level on a video game, do you find it easier to understand what to do if someone:**

A Lets you watch them do it.

B Tells you how to do it, step by step.

2 **Your friend is telling you a story about getting stranded on an island with her family during a boat trip. Would you rather they:**

A Kept to the main facts of the story with just a few extra details.

B Told you every single detail so you can really picture it.

3 **Your parents have said you're allowed to redecorate your room, however you want. Amazing. You just need to let them know how you'd like it to look. Would you:**

A Describe it in a lot of detail.

B Draw them a picture.

4 **Do you find it funnier when your friends put on silly voices and faces or when they tell actual jokes and make puns—such as "One lung said to another... we be-lung together!" (Sorry, that's a terrible one)?**

A A word-based joke (a good one, though…).

B Silly voices and faces.

5 A new girl joins your after-school sport— she introduces herself to everyone but you don't have a chance to talk to her. Before next week, are you more likely to:

A Forget her name but remember her face.

B Forget her face but remember her name.

6 Your parents tell you that you're going on a camping trip a short train trip away, like you normally do in the summer. But when you get to the train station, surprise! You're all actually going to the airport, for a mystery vacation abroad. How do you feel?

A So excited. I love surprises and mysteries—this is such an adventure.

B I want to be excited, but I'm really worried and uncomfortable—I wish they'd told me ahead of time rather than springing it on me now.

7 If there is a sign at the park saying "Keep off the grass," does it make you want to walk on the grass even if you hadn't thought of it before?

A Yes, definitely.

B No, it's against the rules.

8 When you're telling a story, do you gesture with your hands a lot—or even make faces and act out certain parts?

A I might move my hands a little bit, but mostly I just use words to tell the story.

B Absolutely. I don't even realize I'm doing it sometimes.

9 Do you feel like it actually helps you understand things better if you doodle in class while you're listening to the teacher?

A Yes, and it's so annoying that the teacher doesn't believe me and tells me off for it.

B No, I don't really doodle much and if I do it's because I'm bored and not really listening.

10 During the weekend, you want to bake something for your family with a bit of help from your parents. Which would you rather make?

A Something easy, like marshmallow crispy treats, where you don't need to follow a recipe closely and you can experiment with different flavors and decoration.

B Something challenging, like a multi-layer cake, where you have to follow a recipe exactly and get all the preparation and timings right or it won't work properly.

Answers on page 42

Answers

Time to find out whether you have more of a "left-brained" or "right-brained" personality—and what that actually means.

Count up the number of times you've answered "Right" or "Left" to the quiz questions.

1. **A** Right
   B Left

2. **A** Right
   B Left

3. **A** Left
   B Right

4. **A** Left
   B Right

5. **A** Right
   B Left

6. **A** Right
   B Left

7. **A** Right
   B Left

8. **A** Left
   B Right

9. **A** Right
   B Left

10. **A** Right
    B Left

Results

Left-brained

You respond well to rules and systems, and you are happiest when things feel clear and ordered in your own mind and in the world around you. You learn best from detailed written or verbal instructions, and you may well blow people away with your skills in math, science, or languages. You like goals and challenges, but remember that you can take it easy and go your own way sometimes.

Right-brained

Arty and creative, you hate being boxed in by rules and ideas of how things "should" be. You like thinking for yourself and always want to test boundaries. You are a visual learner and a bit of a daydreamer, your thoughts cartwheeling freely around inside your head. Just make sure that people don't feel ignored or let down when your attention is caught by something new.

Left or Right— does it matter?

Of course, we know now that either the left or right side of your brain doesn't actually rule over you. But what is true is that people vary hugely in how they prefer to learn, communicate with others, and respond to rules and order. No preference is good or bad, nor is having no strong preference at all.

In fact, because of the way ideas about "left-brained" and "right-brained" personalities combine a few different attitudes and behaviors, without much in the way of scientific evidence, a final judgment either way doesn't mean a huge amount. For example, you could be a very visual learner (a "right-brained" trait) but feel more comfortable following the rules ("left-brained").

It's best to focus on the answers you've given and how knowing these things about yourself might help you in future. For instance, if doodling helps you concentrate and you'd rather learn by watching someone than by listening to an explanation, you're probably quite a visual learner. Try drawing labeled pictures as part of your revision for a subject, and practice visualizing them and re-creating them from memory. It really works.

Knowing yourself better means you can tailor the way you approach things—from schoolwork to friendships to training in a sport—to what actually fits your personality and ways of thinking. It's like a life hack for your own brain.

Aspects of Personality

Sometimes it might seem like a person is pretty easy to define—a thrill-seeking sports nut, a sour-faced misery guts, a free-thinking hippie—but there's always more to it than that. There are all sorts of different ways of thinking and behaving that come together to create someone's personality, and researchers have developed individual tests to measure many of them. There are four areas that can be particularly helpful in figuring out what makes you tick...

Acting on impulse

Are you happy making decisions on the spot, or do you prefer to carefully consider all your options before committing to anything? If you're saving up for something big, like an expensive video game, do you still find it hard to resist blowing your money on candy every time you pass a store?

The Barratt Impulsiveness Scale was created in 1959 to measure how impulsive someone is—that is, how much they tend to act without really thinking beforehand. The test was updated thirty-six years later and became the BIS-11, a questionnaire that asks the subject how they would behave in various common situations.

People with high impulsiveness scores tend to make snap decisions, without thinking about the consequences. People with low scores like to think things through and not give in to passing feelings. Guess who's more likely to resist the lure of candy and hang on to their savings?

What is empathy?

Empathy is the ability to put yourself in someone else's shoes and understand what they are feeling. It allows you to sense and, to some extent, predict a person's thoughts, feelings, and behaviors. It's the closest thing we have to mind-reading.

Psychologists have broken down the broader idea of "empathy" into separate forms of empathy that people don't necessarily practice all at once: understanding others' feelings, sensing others' feelings and caring about others' feelings.

A number of different empathy tests have been developed, some quite specific to particular thought processes or situations, but the Basic Empathy Scale (BES) looks at overall levels of empathy. It was originally used with young people, but has now also been tested with adults. Empathy is now believed to play a really important role in how communities and societies get along. Makes sense, really, as it's all about caring about others.

Neophiliac or neophobe?

Are you a neophiliac or a neophobe? Or are you just confused by the question?

These terms have been used by researchers to describe people's attitudes toward new things and experiences, which they believe to be an important part of someone's personality.

At one end of the testing scale are the neophiliacs, who find newness exciting and fulfilling; at the other end are the neophobes, who find it uncomfortable and maybe even threatening.

We now live in a world where huge businesses constantly churn out new products—clothes, gadgets, toys, snacks—quicker and in greater numbers than our planet can possibly support. Have we all become neophiliacs, and can we train ourselves out of it to save Earth and ourselves?

Why worry?

Some people seem to worry about almost everything, whereas others appear to drift through life with not a care in the world. Why?

There's no simple answer to that question, but it does appear that some people feel more comfortable accepting that they can't control everything—including what others think of them. Different tests explore what sorts of things people worry about, and how much.

You may have heard people using the term "anxiety"—this is when people worry so much about one particular thing, or lots of different things, that it affects their health and what they feel they can do in life. It's very common but can be a really tricky thing to handle, even for adults, so it's really important that you tell an adult you trust if you feel like you're worrying about things too much.

Barratt Impulsiveness Test

**People with higher levels of impulsiveness might find this
test a bit easier, because you have to make quick decisions.
Try to answer each question within one or two seconds.**

1 **At school, do you wriggle around in your
chair when the teacher talks for a long time?**

A Yes, always.

B Sometimes.

C Not really.

D Never.

2 **Do you ever shout or make a loud noise just
for the sake of it?**

A Yes, all the time.

B Sometimes.

C I can only remember doing it a couple of times.

D No, what would people think?

3 **Have you ever told someone a secret you
weren't supposed to, because it felt like you
couldn't keep it in any longer?**

A No, I would never tell a secret when I'd been asked
not to.

B I really try not to, and I hardly ever do.

C A few times, when it was a big one.

D I spill almost every secret I'm told. I can't resist it.

4 **How often do you change your mind about
what job you want when you're grown up?**

A It feels like I want to do something different almost
every day—whenever I hear about something new.

B I flit between a few different ideas, depending
on my mood.

C I have one main idea, but sometimes if I learn about
a new job I think about doing that instead.

D Never, I know what I want to do and I stick to it.

5 **Does it feel like you have all sorts of
different thoughts racing around your head
at top speed?**

A Not at all, my thoughts feel pretty under control.

B Not really, except for when I get stressed out.

C Quite often, but sometimes my brain slows down and
gives me some peace.

D All the time, it can be exhausting.

6 **If you have a few different chores to do at
home, in which order do you tackle them?**

A If I don't feel like doing them, I won't do them at all—
if I do, I just do each one when I feel like I want to.

B I jump from task to task without any real order, and
I sometimes forget to go back and finish the earlier
ones—oops.

C I try to do them in an order that makes sense,
but as long as they all get done properly I don't
mind too much.

D I plan a set order for the best way to get them done,
and I stick to it and finish them one after another.

7 **If you don't like a movie, do you keep watching
it until the end anyway?**

A Of course, I would never just turn it off part way through.

B I'd have to really, really hate it or find it super boring,
and be watching it alone—and even then I'd probably
keep watching most of the time.

C It depends. If I'm watching it with other people, I'd stick
it out, but if it was just me, I'd probably turn it off.

D Of course not. Why would I keep watching something I did
like?

8 If you won $100, what would you do with the money?

A Spend it, obviously. I'd keep buying whatever I felt like until it was gone.

B I'd like to spend it on something that I'd wanted for a while, but I know I'd spend at least a bit on silly little things I just couldn't resist.

C I'd try to spend some of it but save at least half, that's what I usually do.

D Save it—I hate the idea of buying silly things and then finding it's all gone, so I'd think for a long time about what I wanted to spend it on and make sure I didn't change my mind.

9 Do you like playing complicated board games that have lots of rules and take at least a couple of hours to finish?

A That sounds like my worst nightmare—I get bored trying to learn the rules and end up daydreaming and not listening, so I never get far and then want to quit.

B Occasionally, but I really have to be in the right mood and I might want to stop playing before the game ends.

C Yes, but if they're not that fun I do feel a bit trapped when I'm stuck playing them for ages—but I wouldn't quit if other people still wanted to play.

D Yes, I love them.

10 When you're trying to concentrate on finishing some difficult homework, do you find that other thoughts pop into your head and distract you?

A No, I find it quite easy to focus on one thing at a time and forget about everything else for a while.

B Sometimes, but I just try to ignore them and they go away soon enough.

C Yes, and I try to ignore them but sometimes I end up getting distracted and stop doing my homework for a while.

D Constantly. It feels almost impossible to keep other thoughts away, and I stop and start all the time because I get distracted over and over again.

Answers on page 54

Empathy Scale

How much do you connect with other people's feelings, and how do they affect you? Read the statements below and decide for each one whether you strongly agree or disagree with it, or just agree or disagree a bit.

strongly disagree   disagree a bit   agree a bit   strongly agree

1 I often cry at books, movies, or TV shows.

2 If I tease someone a bit in class and everyone laughs but it seems like that person is upset, I feel really bad.

3 If a teacher gave two of my classmates detention for fighting, even though one person was being a bully and the other one was sticking up for themselves, it would make me angry.

4 If someone really loves a present I've given them, it makes me happier than getting a present myself.

5 It makes me really angry or upset when I see someone shouting at their dog or pulling it roughly on its leash.

6 If I think I've hurt a friend's feelings, I find it hard to stop worrying about it.

7 It makes me really sad when I see homeless people on the street.

8 I love watching online videos of people's happy moments, like being reunited with their pets, because it makes me feel happy too.

9 If I didn't really care much about a school trip but everyone in my class got really excited about it, it would make me feel more excited too.

10 If I saw a new person in my class helping someone with a difficult problem and being kind to them when they felt frustrated, it would make me want to be their friend.

Answers on page 54

Neophilia Quiz

Are you all about the new new new, or do you crave familiarity? This quiz tests how much you enjoy all kinds of new things and experiences.

1 Do you like trying out all sorts of different after-school activities that you end up quitting, or do you stick to a couple and keep going for years and years?

A Stick to a few and keep them up.

B Try lots, quit lots.

2 Do you get bored studying the same book in class for a long time, or do you like really getting into it in depth?

A Soooo bored.

B I prefer it to rushing through books.

3 Would you rather have a best friend who was really fun and adventurous, but sometimes a bit mean, or one who was more cautious but very caring and loyal?

A Fun and adventurous.

B Caring and loyal.

4 Do you often try to persuade your parents to let you stay up later, because there are better things you could be doing than sleeping?

A No, I'm happy being cozy in bed.

B Yes, all the time.

5 When you walk around your school between classes, do you ever take a different route just for the sake of it—even if it's longer?

A No, why would I do that?

B Yes, it's so boring always going the same way.

6 **It's your birthday! How are you celebrating?**

A A party with all your favorite foods and games, and your closest friends.

B A big surprise party, or an activity you've never done before.

7 **Do you listen to the same songs over and over again, or do you quickly get sick of a song if you listen to it more than a few times?**

A I can keep listening to my favorites for ages and still love them.

B I go quickly from loving a song to hating it if I listen to it too much.

8 **When you grow up, do you want to stay in your home country, or move somewhere different?**

A I might want to travel, but I don't think I'd like actually living in another country.

B I definitely want to try living somewhere else. It's a big wide world—why not explore?

9 **If you saw someone doing something that looked fun but dangerous, like making a big jump between two walls, would you want to try it too?**

A Yes, what's the point in life if you don't take chances sometimes?

B No, I'll leave other people to break their legs doing stupid things.

10 **Do you often get bored with all of your clothes and feel like you don't want to wear any of them?**

A Yep, I'm always asking for new clothes.

B No, I have my favorite comfy things and I wear them until my parents insist they're too worn out.

Answers on page 55

Why Worry? Quiz

Do you float through life with not a care in the world, or are you always worrying about what could go wrong? Take this quiz to find out how much of a worrier you might really be.

1 **If you thought one of your friends seemed a bit cold or grumpy, would you think you'd done something wrong and that they didn't like you anymore?**

A Definitely, and I'd feel really panicked.

B Probably, and I'd worry about it and want to ask them.

C I don't think so, but I'd try to remember if I'd done anything to upset them.

D No, it could be about anything.

2 **When you have a test coming up, do you get so nervous that you find it hard to relax or sleep?**

A Always, even if I've prepared for it—it's horrible and I worry it makes me do worse in the test.

B Sometimes, especially in subjects I find difficult.

C I get a bit nervous if I know I haven't revised enough.

D No, what's the point? Revise or don't, then just get it over with.

3 **If you walked into the classroom and some of your classmates stopped their conversation, would you assume they had been saying mean things about you?**

A Definitely, and it would be all I could think about for the rest of the class.

B Probably, and I would feel awkward about it.

C Maybe, but if I didn't like them, I wouldn't really care.

D No, everything isn't always about me—and who cares what they say anyway?

4 **Do you find sports like BMXing and skateboarding scary or exciting?**

A Terrifying! I can't even bear to watch, in case someone gets hurt.

B Pretty scary. I wouldn't do it myself, but I quite like watching it.

C Exciting. I'd like to be good at them, but the advanced tricks are kind of scary.

D Exciting, of course. I want to be able to do all the most impressive tricks.

5 **If someone else in your year at school had the same birthday as you, would you move your party to another day in case everyone decided to go to theirs instead—even if you didn't have that many friends in common?**

A Definitely—I already didn't want a party in case nobody came, but my parents made me.

B Probably, I'd feel bad if more people did go to theirs.

C No, but I'd worry a bit that fewer people would come to mine.

D Of course not, even if we did have the same friends—people can choose whichever party they like.

6 **If you got a haircut that you weren't sure suited you, would you feel worried about going into school in case people made fun of it?**

A Obviously—I'd pretend to be sick for a few days so it had time to grow back a bit.

B Yes, I'd feel awful going into school the next day.

C A bit, but these things happen—and hair grows!

D No, who cares? It's just hair. Let them make fun if they want, but more likely no one will notice.

7 **Do you daydream about things that you don't want to happen, like your parents making you move to a new house and go to a different school, and then worry about them, even if there's no reason to think they'll ever happen?**

A Always, and the ideas get stuck in my head and make me feel panicky.

B Sometimes, and it's not very nice.

C Not really, but I might think about things like that if they've just happened to someone I know.

C No, what's the point in worrying about things that haven't happened and you can't control?

8 **At a school dance, do you prefer to hang around talking because you worry that you might not be a good dancer?**

A Absolutely, I'd never dance under any circumstances.

B I prefer talking, but I might dance a bit in a group so I don't stand out.

C I like dancing—I can feel self-conscious at first, but it gets better after a while.

D Never. It doesn't matter what you look like—dancing is supposed to be fun!

9 **Have you ever wanted to join in with doing something, like diving into the swimming pool from the high board, but just watched in the end because you got too nervous?**

A All the time—I feel like I'll just never be brave enough to do those things.

B A few times, but sometimes I can make myself try it.

C Only once or twice, when it seemed really difficult or dangerous.

D No, I'm the one trying to get everyone else to do stuff like that.

10 **Do you think a lot about the future, and try to make sure things don't turn out differently from how you want them to?**

A Constantly, and I worry about all the things that are out of my control too.

B Quite a lot—I try to focus on working hard, and try to make all the right decisions.

C Sometimes, but you never know what might happen, so I try to focus on the present.

D No, what's the point? Anything could happen and things will work out, one way or another.

Answers on page 55

Answers

Impulsiveness quiz

So, how impulsive are you?
Let's find out...

For questions 1, 2, 4, 6, 8, and 9:

A = 4 points

B = 3 points

C = 2 points

D = 1 point

For questions 3, 5, 7, and 10:

A = 1 point

B = 2 points

C = 3 points

D = 4 points

Add up your points for each answer to find out your overall impulsiveness score.

0–17: Not impulsive at all

Plans and promises mean a lot to you, and once you've said you'll do something, you don't change your mind. You're also more comfortable knowing what's in store, rather than having to figure it out as you go along. But remember that your instincts can tell you important truths—even ones as simple as "You're allowed to have some fun, too."

18–25: Not very impulsive

You like making plans and you mostly try to stick to them, but sometimes you let yourself do what you want in the moment. Your reliability and self-discipline should help you to achieve your goals, but remember that it's good to cut loose sometimes.

26–33: Kind of impulsive

You trust your instincts and make quick decisions, which can help keep you on track for a life that feels fun and right for you. But remember that it's okay to take a moment to think things through or see how they turn out, without rushing into anything new—sometimes it's all a bit clearer once the dust has had a chance to settle.

34–40: Very impulsive

You're so super spontaneous, it's a miracle you managed to stick around long enough to finish this quiz. You like your life to be free and exciting, lived according to however you feel in the moment. You're probably a really fun person to have around, but be careful not to disappoint people who care more about plans and promises than you might.

Empathy quiz

Where do you sit on the empathy scale?

For each of your responses, score yourself as follows:

Strongly agree = + 2 points

Agree a bit = + 1 point

Disagree a bit = -1 point

Strongly disagree = - 2 points

Check out where your total score is on the empathy scale:

-20 -15 -10 -5 0 5 10 15 20

Closest to -20:

Whoa, empathy-free zone. You look out for number one and expect others to do the same. Sounds like it might get a bit lonely…

Closest to -10:

You aren't completely cold to how other people are feeling, but it may seem that way to others. Try putting yourself in other people's shoes sometimes; you could learn a lot from it.

Closest to 0:

You care about others but you might not like connecting to your feelings too much. Remember that it's a strength, not a weakness, to feel and express emotions—keep in touch with them.

Closest to 10:

Your mood is affected quite strongly by how other people feel—but it doesn't necessarily make or break your day. You have a sense of what is right and wrong, so make sure to follow through with actions that put good out into the world.

Closest to 20:

You have an extremely strong sense of how people should treat one another, and you can feel overwhelmed by others' feelings. Remember that you can't be responsible for everyone's happiness—and that you need to look after yourself, too.

Neophilia quiz

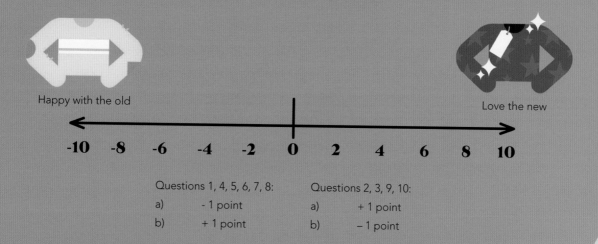

Happy with the old

Love the new

-10 -8 -6 -4 -2 0 2 4 6 8 10

Questions 1, 4, 5, 6, 7, 8:
a)   - 1 point
b)   + 1 point

Questions 2, 3, 9, 10:
a)   + 1 point
b)   − 1 point

Worries quiz

Mostly A

You worry a lot, as do many people—both children and adults. You know that worrying doesn't really change anything, but that doesn't make it any easier to stop sometimes, does it? Talk with your a parent, carer, teacher, or another adult you trust—they have a few more years' experience dealing with worries, and they should be able to help you deal with them and not feel those horrible moments of panic so often.

Mostly B

You worry quite a bit—maybe more than you'd like to. Worrying is one of the ways your brain tries to keep you safe, by thinking about the possible bad consequences of your actions, but it can go into overdrive and end up not feeling very helpful at all. This is particularly true if we have no control over the things we're worrying about. Talk to an adult you trust if your worries feel like they're getting too much to handle.

Mostly C

You worry about things now and then, but it doesn't tend to stop you from doing what you want to do. You know about risks, but you also know that things can go well—and usually do. Worrying about things you can control can push you to make good choices, but you know there is a lot that is out of your hands, too.

Mostly D

Wow, has a worry ever crossed your mind? Many people would feel very lucky to have your laid-back attitude to life—remember to be sensitive to the fact that others struggle with worries that might not make sense to you. And don't forget that you're not immune to danger, so avoid taking big risks even if you aren't worried about them.

Intelligence

What do you think of as intelligence? Is it knowing all sorts of facts, understanding long and difficult books, or maybe being able to figure out solutions to problems you've never seen before? Throughout history, there have been lots of (sometimes questionable) ideas about what intelligence is and how to measure it.

Today, the Intelligence Quotient (IQ) Test is the best-known way of measuring intelligence. It gives you a score based on how many questions you answer correctly, and how advanced that is for your age. But many people think that it's impossible to boil down someone's intelligence to a single number, and that IQ tests don't really mean that much.

Different studies have linked a variety of personality traits—both positive and negative—to high levels of intelligence, but the results aren't very consistent. One of the stronger links is that people with higher IQ scores apparently tend to be more open to new experiences.

Fluid and crystallized intelligence

The psychologist Raymond Cattell thought that intelligence is made up of different abilities that work together and affect each other. He described two kinds of intelligence in particular: fluid intelligence and crystallized intelligence.

Fluid intelligence is a person's ability to reason and solve problems by identifying patterns and thinking logically, without having any particular knowledge or past experience of the problem in hand.

Crystallized intelligence is a person's ability to use the knowledge, experience, and skills that they've gained over their lifetime.

Adults generally have higher levels of crystallized intelligence than children, because they've had longer to learn things—makes sense, right? But adults shouldn't be too cocky—children have a lot of fluid intelligence, which for adults drops off considerably by middle age. Tell a grown up that. They'll LOVE it.

Culture-Fair IQ Test

Some types of tests—including most of the exams that you'll take at school—are designed to measure your crystallized intelligence: the facts and skills that you've managed to pick up and remember. Those who have had more advantages in life—such as a good education and lots of opportunities to visit museums and read tons of books—tend to do better on these kinds of tests.

Unfair? Raymond Cattell thought so. He developed the Culture-Fair IQ Test to measure people's fluid intelligence, which doesn't seem to be as linked to people's life experiences. He aimed to make it fairer than other IQ tests by deliberately avoiding any questions where cultural or educational differences might affect people's scores.

Many people now think that there are different forms of intelligence—someone might be amazing at solving math problems, but not so great with words. In this chapter, you'll have a chance to test yourself in a few different areas and see where your strengths might lie.

Verbal Reasoning Quiz

Are you a whiz with words? Or do you suffer through spelling, groan at grammar, and cry at comprehension? Either way, try these verbal reasoning questions and see how you do.

Remember, if English is not your first language or you have a learning difficulty such as dyslexia, these tests won't really be fair for you. Try it for fun, but don't worry about the results—it's the test's fault, not yours!

Choose the opposites

1 Proud   **A** Happy   **B** Ashamed   **C** Angry

2 Expensive   **A** Ugly   **B** Fashionable   **C** Cheap

3 Calm   **A** Stressed   **B** Cruel   **C** Peaceful

Spelling

Which is the correct spelling of each word?

4   **A** Gitar   **B** Guitar   **C** Gittar

5   **A** Weird   **B** Wierd   **C** Weired

6   **A** Menshun   **B** Mention   **C** Mension

Hidden words

Find the four-letter word that is made from the first two letters of one word and last two letters of another. The words don't need to be next to each other.

For example, in: Dare   Also   Grow
The hidden word is...real!

7   Lion   Lying   Tiger

8   Fang   Mask   Into

9   Fluff   Moat   Cry

Comprehension

Read the paragraph below and answer questions about the information it gives you.

Spanish is the forth most widely spoken language in the world. Over 400 million people speak Spanish, and it is an official language of 21 different countries around the world. There are some differences between how people speak Spanish in different countries—for example, in Spain the word for "juice" is "zumo," but in Spanish-speaking countries in the Americas it is usually called "jugo."

10 **The most widely spoken language in the world has more than 400 million speakers.**

    A True.

    B False.

    C Cannot tell.

11 **In Spain, "juice" is usually called "zumo."**

    A True.

    B False.

    C Cannot tell.

12 **Some countries in Africa have Spanish as an official language.**

    A True.

    B False.

    C Cannot tell.

Which sentence is correct?

Decide whether Sentence A or Sentence B is correct—or whether neither of them are.

13 **A** They had a great time at the movies and was happy to share a bag of popcorn between them.

    B They had a great time at the movies and were happy to share a bag of popcorn between them.

    C Neither.

14 **A** Dana walked really quick to school so she wouldn't be late.

    B Dana walks really quickly to school so she wouldn't be late.

    C Neither.

15 **A** I prefer studying at you're house because it's quieter.

    B I prefer studying at your house because it's quieter.

    C Neither.

Answers on page 68

Numerical Reasoning Quiz

Math isn't everyone's favorite class at school, but getting your head around numbers can help you do all sorts of things—from quickly figuring out how much candy the loose change in your pockets will buy you to unraveling the scientific mysteries of the universe! Test your math mastery by trying to answer these questions...

If you have dyscalculia (often called "number dyslexia"), remember that this test won't really be fair for you. The Culture-Fair IQ Test on pages 64–67 has more suitable questions based around spotting patterns and rules, which is a really important part of math too.

Mental arithmetic

Do the following sums in your head, without writing down any working-out or using a calculator. Make a note of your answer for each question, though, so you don't forget it!

1 ? + 36 = 41

2 6 x ? = 36

3 ? − 70 = 31

4 7 x 8 = ?

5 66 ÷ ? = 11

What comes next?

Complete the sequence by figuring out the pattern and filling in the missing number. Don't use a calculator, but you can write down your working-out on a piece of paper.

6	7	14	21	28	?
7	20	41	62	83	?
8	80	40	20	10	?
9	30	45	60	75	?
10	2	6	14	30	?

Number problems

For each problem, figure out the right answer without using a calculator. You can write down your working-out on a piece of paper.

If English isn't your first language or you have a learning difficulty such as dyslexia, the wordy nature of these questions might make them unfair for you. So feel free to just mark yourself on the first two sections of this quiz to get a more accurate score.

11 **If a bag of chips costs 60 cents, how much would five bags cost?**

A $3.00

B $2.60

C $2.20

12 **If 20 people each gave $5.00 a month to a charity for a year, how much money in total would the charity receive?**

A $500

B $1,000

C $1,200

13 **If one shopping bag can hold five boxes of chocolates, how many shopping bags would you need to carry twenty-two boxes of chocolates?**

A 4

B 5

C 6

14 **If a factory produces five toys a minute, how many can it produce in an hour?**

A 200

B 300

C 500

15 **If fifty pens cost $5.00, how much should twenty pens cost?**

A $2.00

B $2.50

C $3.00

Answers on page 68

Spatial Reasoning Quiz

Have you got a knack for arranging things so they fit together just right? Can you think of a shape and twist it around in your head to see it every which way? Then you might be a spatial genius. Let's find out...

Rotating keys

Imagine rotating these funny-looking keys so they face in a different direction, but don't otherwise change in any way. Which option—A, B, or C—looks correct?

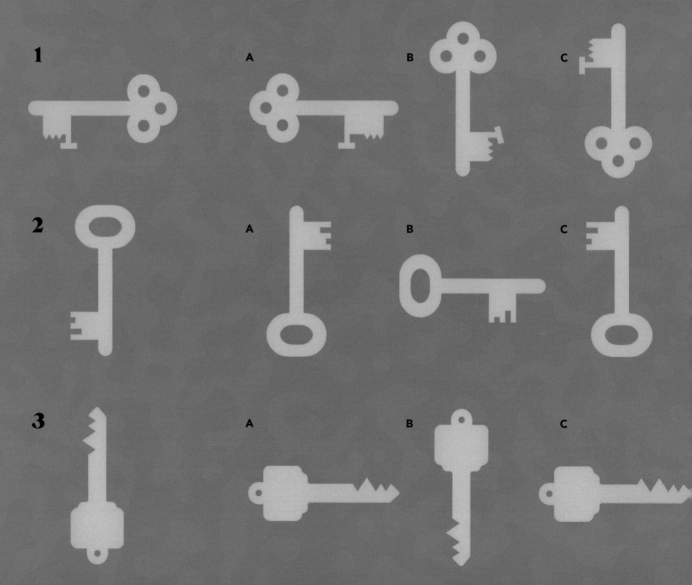

View from the top

For these questions, you need to imagine that you're looking at a colorful 3-D pyramid from directly above so that it seems flat. Which option—A, B, or C—is the correct view?

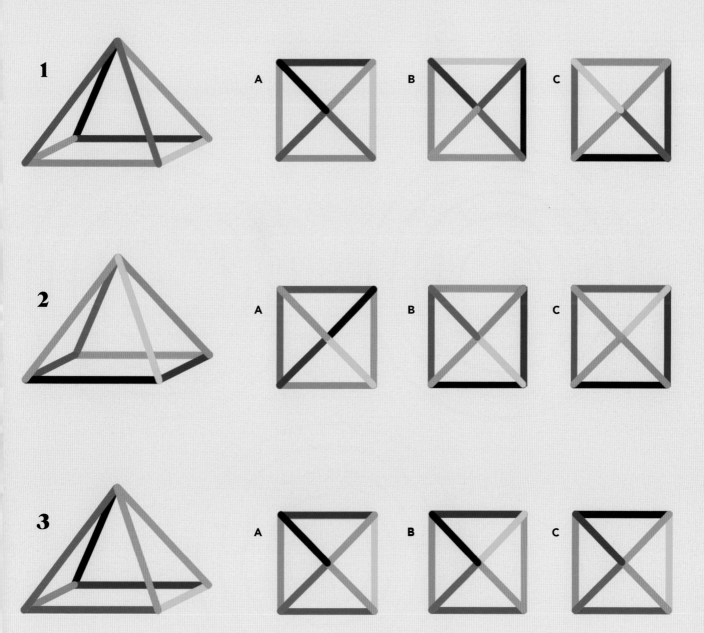

Answers on page 69

Culture-Fair IQ Test

This quiz tests your abstract reasoning skill—which means it's all about figuring out patterns and rules, without using math, English, or general knowledge. It's just you and your brain. Enjoy!

Mazes

Set a timer for thirty seconds and try to solve each maze before the timer goes off. Make a note about which you solved so you can remember when it's time to figure out your score.

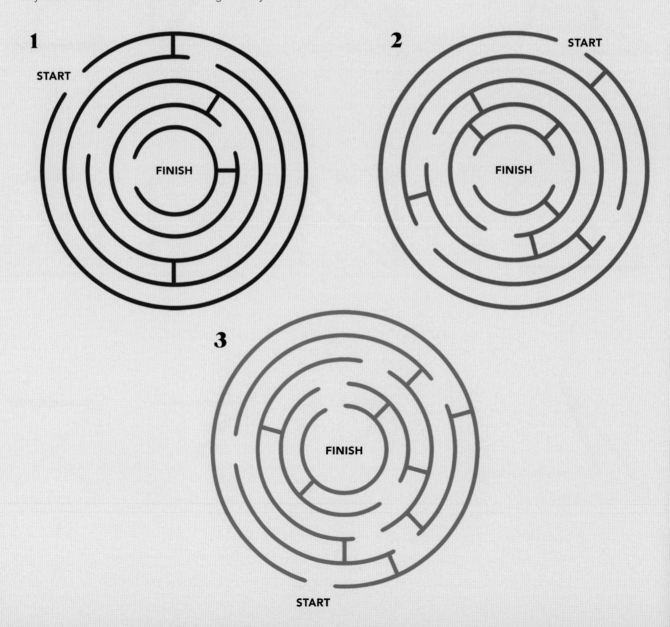

Which one matches?

Which shape in the bottom row matches best with the three shapes in the top row?

4

A

B

C

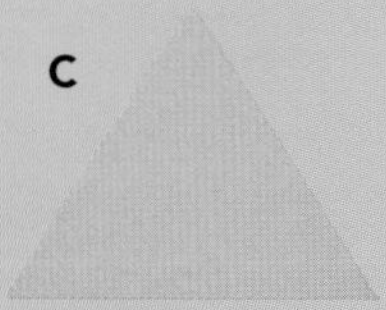

5

A

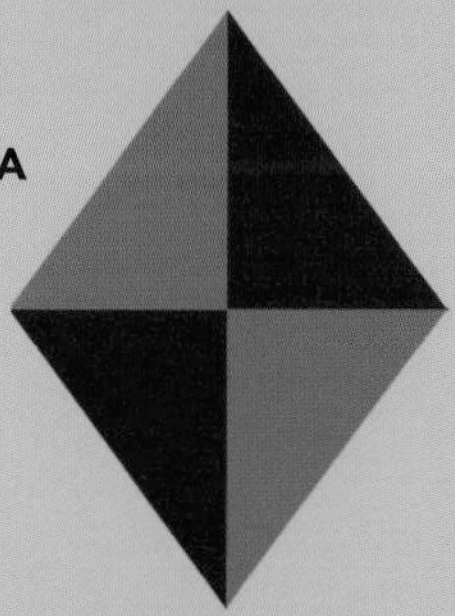

B

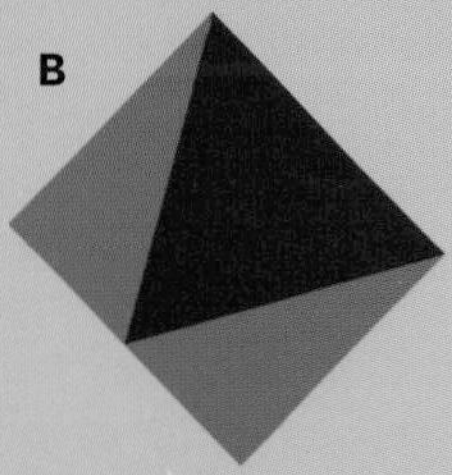

C

6

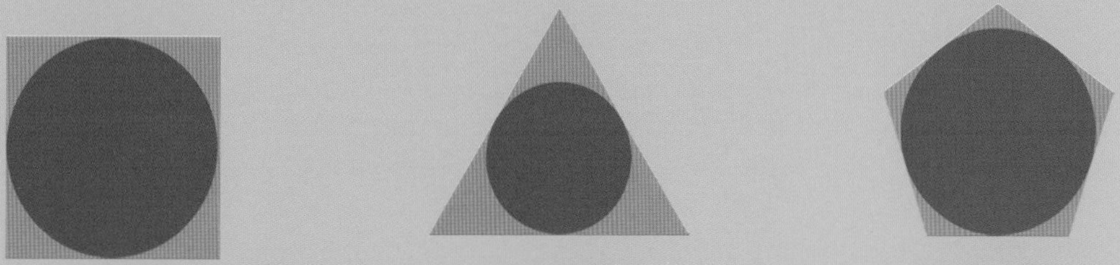

A

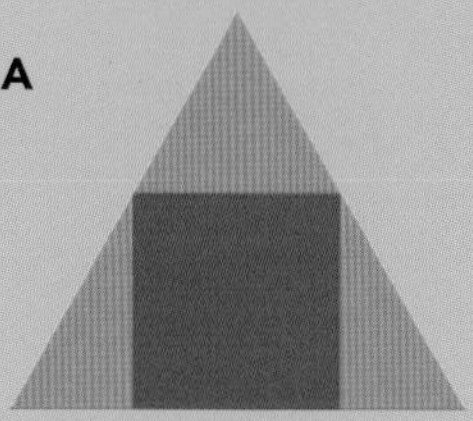

B

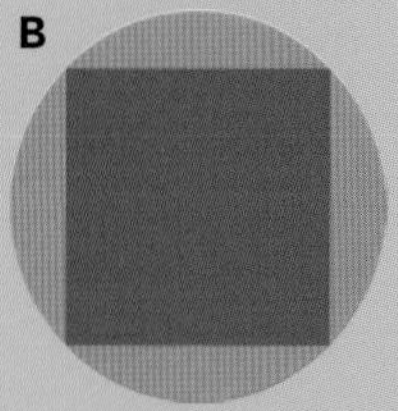

C

If this, then that...

Look at the change between the top left example shape in each grid and the one just below it. Then, applying the same rule to the next example shape, pick option A, B, C, or D to fill in the empty square.

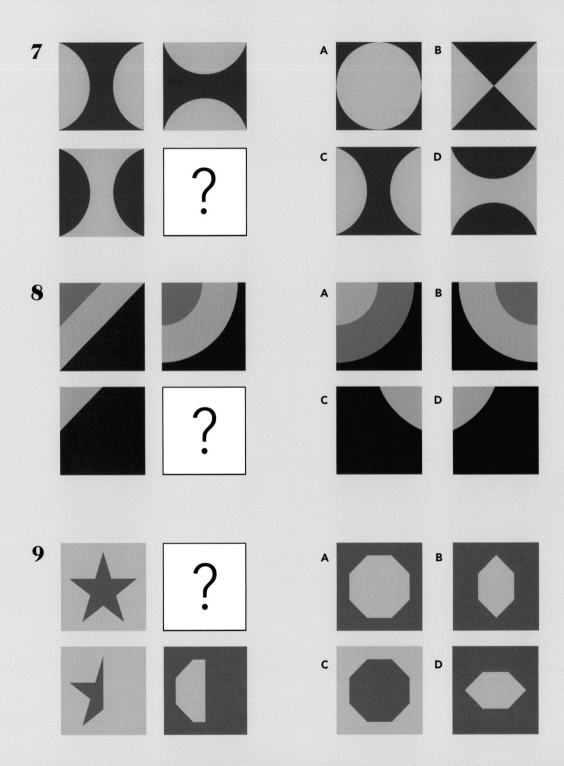

What comes next?

Try to figure out the pattern in each top row of shapes, and pick option A, B, or C to complete the sequence.

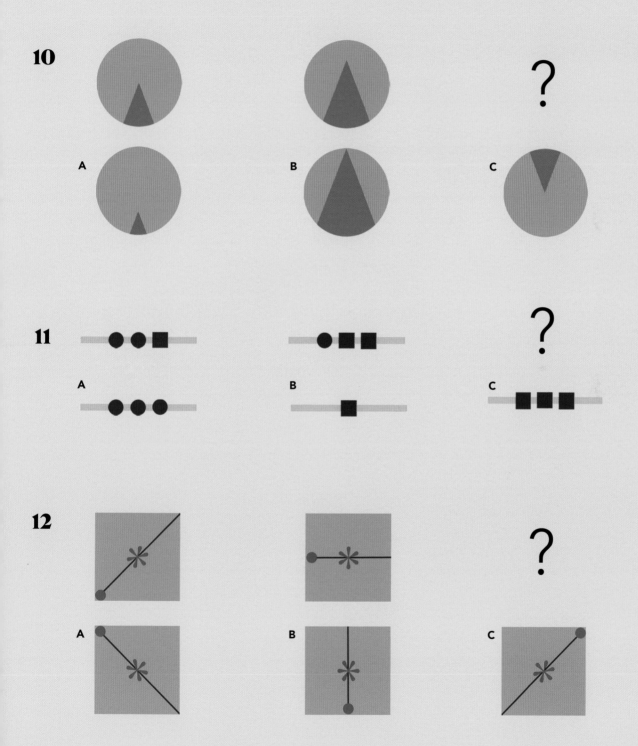

Answers

All right, smarty-pants, let's find out how you did!

Verbal reasoning quiz

Every correct answer earns 2 points—what's your total score, out of a possible 30?

Circle the opposites

1. B
2. C
3. A

Spelling

4. B
5. A
6. B

Hidden words

7. only
8. skin
9. flat

Comprehension

10. A—True—if Spanish is the forth most widely spoken language in the world, and it has over 400 million speakers, then the most widely spoken language must have even more speakers.
11. A—True
12. C—Cannot tell—the paragraph mentions that there are Spanish-speaking countries around the world, but the only areas it mentions by name are Spain and the Americas.

Which sentence is correct?

13. B
14. C
15. B

Numerical reasoning quiz

Again, give yourself 2 points for each correct answer—what's your score out of a possible 30? How does it compare to your verbal reasoning score?

Mental arithmetic

1. 5
2. 6
3. 101
4. 56
5. 6

What comes next?

6. 35—it's the 7 times table
7. 104—you add 21 each time
8. 5—you divide by 2 each time
9. 90—you add 15 each time
10. 62—you multiply by 2 and add 2 each time (tricky)

Number problems

11. A—$0.60 x 5 = $3.00
12. C—20 x $5 = $100 per month. There are 12 months in a year, so $100 x 12 = $1,200
13. B—20 of the boxes fit exactly into 4 bags, but you need an extra bag for the 2 left over
14. B—There are 60 minutes in an hour, so 5 x 60 = 300
15. A—If 50 pens cost $5.00, you can divide both numbers by 5 to find that 10 pens cost $1.00. Double the pens means double the cost, so multiply the cost of 10 pens by 2 to find the cost of 20 pens—tricky!

Spatial reasoning quiz

For this quiz, give yourself 5 points for each correct answer—what's your score out of 30 this time? How does it compare with your verbal and numerical reasoning scores?

Rotating keys

1. C—Key B doesn't have the correct teeth, and Key A has them on the wrong side

2. A—Key B doesn't have the correct teeth, and Key C has them on the wrong side

3. A—Key C doesn't have the correct teeth, and Key B has them on the wrong side

View from the top

1. A
2. B
3. A—tricky!

Culture-Fair IQ Test

A full-length IQ test will give you an IQ number based on your answers across a huge range of questions, and how that score compares with the average score for your age. As this is a short and sweet version of a culture-fair IQ test, it wouldn't be accurate to give you an IQ number based on your results.

Instead, you'll get a score for your abstract reasoning skills, which is what you're testing here. Award yourself 1 point for each correct answer, then multiply your total by 100 and divide it by your age to get your final score. We're not in the numerical reasoning quiz anymore, so do feel free to use a calculator.

Mazes

Give yourself a point for each maze that you managed to solve within the time limit. (There should be a tick beside those ones, and a cross beside the ones you didn't finish.)

Which one matches?

4. A—it has four sides
5. C—it is made up of two triangles
6. C—it has a circle in the middle

If this, then that...

If you didn't get the right answer, look at the question again and try to figure out why it wasn't right—it can help you get the hang of it for the future.

7. D
8. D
9. A

What comes next?

Again, if you didn't get the right answer, look back at the question and try to figure out why it doesn't fit in the sequence.

10. B
11. C
12. A

Creativity

Do you think of yourself as a "creative type"? And what exactly does that mean to you—someone who's great at drawing or writing songs, or maybe just a daydreamer who sees the world a bit differently from everyone else?

Everyone has the ability to be creative, but some people appear to be particularly good at coming up with original ideas and ways of expressing themselves. Rather than there being a single "creative personality" type, experts have found that highly creative people tend to have a handy combination of different personality traits.

Creative traits

One of the personality traits most closely linked to creativity is "openness to new experiences." This is one of the Big Five traits (see page 33) often used by psychologists today in personality testing.

Makes sense, right? To come up with original ideas, you have to be willing to think about things in different ways, rather than sticking to what you already know. Also, ideas don't come out of thin air— your brain knits them together from the various strands of information it has taken in from the world around you. So the more new experiences you're open to, the more material your brain has to work with.

People who are more willing to persevere and risk making mistakes also tend to be more creative. First, because it means they are more likely to put in time and effort to develop skills and learn information that they can use in new and interesting ways. Secondly, because translating a creative idea into something that others can experience often takes a few tries—even the most creative people have to push through some real stinkers of ideas to get to their greatest ones.

The creative process

So what exactly is your brain doing when you're trying to come up with genius new ideas? Experts tend to divide up its creative process into four stages: preparation, incubation, illumination, and verification. The good news: you need to relax—at least for a little while—for your brain to do its best work.

1. Preparation

This stage is all about absorbing knowledge for your brain to play around with, coming up with the new connections that turn into creative thoughts. Read, watch, explore, and examine—and think about writing notes, making sketches, and building mind maps to help you organize your first impressions.

2. Incubation

This stage gives your brain time to make new connections based on the knowledge it has just absorbed. Most of what goes on in your brain happens on a subconscious level, without you actively controlling it, and by relaxing you actually make it easier for your brain to develop creative ideas.

3. Illumination

When your brain recognizes that it might have come up with a new connection that could be useful to you, you may have a "lightbulb moment" as this thought or idea suddenly pings into your conscious brain. Eureka!

4. Verification

Coming up with a creative idea isn't the end of the story. At first it might be vague or unclear, so you'll need to refine it with further thinking and hard work. Only then will you be able to tell if it's really a good idea, and develop it to a point where you can present it to others and persuade them it's good too.

Guilford's Alternative Uses Test

Around seventy years ago, an American psychologist named J. P. Guilford developed an idea for a test to measure a person's creativity. It was new, it was radical, it was...to hand someone a paper clip and ask them to come up with as many different uses for it as possible. Seriously!

To be fair, testing for creativity is a tricky business. Guilford wanted to test how differently someone could think, rather than how good they were at answering questions correctly, and that's much tougher to measure. Try this Alternative Uses test, and find out how creative you can be...

How it works

1 If you can, gather at least two more people to take the test with you. You'll see why when you finish the test and head to the Answers page.

2 Pick three of the objects listed on the next page. If you're taking the test as a group, you all need to agree to pick the same three objects.

3 See how many different uses you can come up with for each object—the more unusual, the better. For a paper clip, for example, "unclogging the hole in a salt shaker" would be a better answer than "holding two sheets of paper together." Give a time limit of fifteen minutes if you want, or leave it more open.

Guilford's original test was quite strict: each use had to be realistic and practical, or it was disqualified. But you can let things be a bit freer and more fun. For example, that paper clip could be a teeny-tiny crutch for a mouse with a sore leg.

This test is pretty simple—but not necessarily easy. Why not try giving yourself the best chance possible by working through the four creative stages on page 71 to come up with your answers?

pencil

brick

leaf

spoon

chair

umbrella

1

Spend a full five minutes looking at the items, studying what they look like close up and from different angles.

2

Leave the items for around fifteen minutes, and do something relaxing and fun.

3

Now look at the items again and write down whatever comes to mind. Stay as relaxed as possible—maybe sit somewhere comfy—and remember that it doesn't matter if the uses seem obvious or silly. When your brain feels completely emptied of ideas, go over your list and circle the three uses you think are the most original.

4

Spend fifteen minutes thinking about how you would actually make these three ideas work, and preparing a thirty-second pitch for each one to explain them to someone else.

rubber band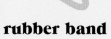

plastic bag

book

shoe

Answers on page 76

Torrance Tests of Creative Thinking

Today, most experts believe that there are different types of creativity—a person might be a wildly creative inventor, but get completely stuck making up a story beyond "Once upon a time…" We often don't appreciate how creative we are, and many psychologists are now exploring "everyday creativity"— the ways we all find to solve new problems and express new thoughts, whatever the day brings.

The Torrance Tests of Creative Thinking—named after their creator, Ellis Paul Torrance— aim to measure how people solve all sorts of different problems in original ways. These tests come together to give an overall score for someone's creativity, but also show where their particular creative strengths lie.

Try the questions on the next page—and remember, there are no wrong answers. Let your imagination run wild and see where it takes you. Try to get another couple of friends or family members to take this test with you—it helps with scoring the answers, and it can be really interesting to see how differently from you they might think.

1 Trace these incomplete shapes onto a piece of paper—then turn them into anything you like.

2 Just suppose…you could breathe underwater. What would you do and where would you go?

3 You're walking down the street when suddenly your shoes vanish. What would you do?

4 Is your backpack sometimes really heavy with all the stuff you have to take to school? Think of some ideas to help solve this everyday problem—and remember, they can be totally out-there or super high-tech if you want.

5 Make up a story about a dog that can play the guitar. Or, if you don't like that story idea, come up with one of your own.

6 What would make this toy robot more fun to play with?

7 Trace this circle five times and this square three times. Cut out the paper shapes and use paper clips to arrange them in as many different ways as possible.

8 You can ask this owl five questions about her life—what do you want to know? Make five guesses about what her life is like.

9 Draw five bean shapes on a piece of paper. Now make up five different drawings based around the shapes— they can be anything, except for beans.

10 Draw a person by using only one kind of shape—circles, triangles, squares, or any other shape you like.

Turn the page to find out what your answers mean

Answers

So, are you the world's next genius inventor, master artist, or storyteller extraordinaire? Let's find out!

Guilford's Alternative Uses test

Creativity tests are notoriously difficult to judge and score. Guilford came up with four criteria—fluency, flexibility, elaboration, and originality—to try to more objectively measure how creative people's answers to this test are.

If you've taken the test along with other people, mark each other's answers—and when it comes to the "originality" score, compare everyone's answers and give points according to whether or not other people have thought of it too.

If you've done the test by yourself, ask someone else to look at your answers—you can't really score yourself fairly in this test. To find out your "originality" score, the person marking your answers will need to have a quick go at the test themselves before they look at yours—you get 1 point for every use they didn't think of.

Fluency

How many different uses have you thought of? You receive 1 point for every different use.

Flexibility

How many different areas do your answers cover? For example, making a ring or a shoe decoration from a paper clip both belong to one area—they're both accessories. But if you suggested using a paper clip to pick a lock, that would be a different area. You receive 1 point for each different area.

Elaboration

What is the level of detail in your answers? For example, if your answer was to use a paper clip "to pick up crumbs from the table" that would be worth more than "to poke a hole through something." You receive up to 3 points for each answer, based on the level of detail:
1= very basic detail;
2 = quite detailed;
3 = very detailed.

Originality

How uncommon are the uses that you've thought of? You'll need at least one other person's answers to compare against for this measurement. You receive up to 3 points for each use.

If comparing with a group: 1 = common (more than one other person in the group has given this answer); 2 = less common (one other person has given it); 3 = uncommon (no one else has given it).

If comparing with only the person scoring: 1 = common (the person scoring got this answer too); 2 = less common (they didn't get this answer, but it's similar to one they wrote); 3 = uncommon (they didn't get this answer or anything close to it).

Torrance Tests for Creativity

The Torrance tests are based on the ideas behind Guilford's Alternative Uses test, but the scoring system is a little different, as the questions each focus on different creative challenges.

If you didn't do this with other people, make sure that the person marking your test has a go at it themselves before they look at your answers. They'll need to compare your answers against theirs to figure out your "originality" score.

Fluency (only applies to Questions 2, 3, 4, 6, and 7)

How many different uses have you thought of? You receive 1 point for every different use.

Originality (all questions)

How uncommon are the uses that you've given as answers? Receive up to 3 points per answer, according to the marking advice given for the Guilford Alternative Uses test.

Elaboration (all questions)

How detailed are your answers? You receive up to 3 points:
1= very basic detail; 2 = quite detailed; 3 = very detailed.

What's your total score? The highest possible number of points suggests the most creative answers—but see which questions you scored highest in to find out your particular creative strengths.

Personality at Work

You might not want to hear this, but when you grow up, you're probably going to spend around a third of your life at work. Yeah, sorry about that...

So it makes sense to at least have a job that you like, right? That you find interesting and rewarding and maybe even kind of fun, and that you're good at, too?

Well, a psychologist named John L. Holland thought so—and he spent his life investigating how someone's personality can predict what kind of job will best suit them. His theory was that most people fit into one of six personality types:

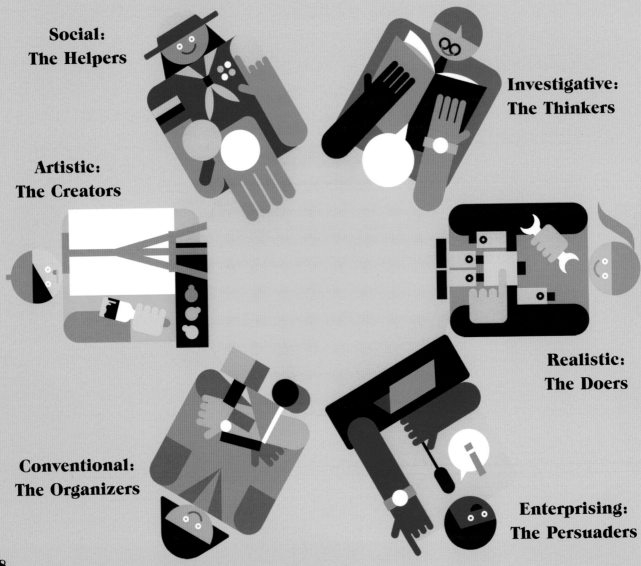

Social:
The Helpers

Investigative:
The Thinkers

Artistic:
The Creators

Realistic:
The Doers

Conventional:
The Organizers

Enterprising:
The Persuaders

Ever heard the phrase "the people make the place"? Holland was a big believer that when people of a certain type came together in a workplace, they created an environment that had its own sort of personality.

So a bunch of Artistic people will create a working environment that supports and rewards the kind of creative thinking that is their shared preference and strength. On the other hand, a group of Conventional people will create an organized environment, ordered by the rules and processes that they find really helpful.

Neither one is better or worse, but put people in the wrong sort of working environment for them and they'll HATE it, and won't do their best work at all. For example, Artistic people will feel stifled and bored in a Conventional environment, and their creativity and free thinking won't be seen as a positive thing.

I mean, if you need someone to organize a lot of important business records, it's probably not SUPER helpful for them to interpretative-dance their way around the room as part of the process…

Holland's handy hexagon

Holland created a handy hexagon model to show which personality types he believed would work best or worst together in different working environments. You can see that the Conventional and Artistic segments are direct opposites, as far away from each other as possible. Each type's closest neighbors are the ones that they might mix with the best—for example, an Artistic type might enjoy having a good, long think with the Investigative types.

Of course, people are much too complicated to fit into one of six personality types—Holland knew that, and said so himself. But he felt that this model could guide people in a direction that would give them and their work the best chance to really shine.

Strong Interest Inventory

The Strong Interest Inventory was first developed in the 1920s, to help people who'd left the military figure out which jobs might suit them. But don't worry, it's been updated—there isn't so much call nowadays for silent-movie actors and telegram operators...

The modern version used around the world is based on the six personality types described by Holland, and tries to figure out how interested you are in different subjects and activities.

So, are you a thinker or a doer? Would you rather help or organize? Get creative or be persuasive? And what does any of it mean for the kind of job that might suit you best? Find out your "type," then turn to pages 82–83 to see into your future...

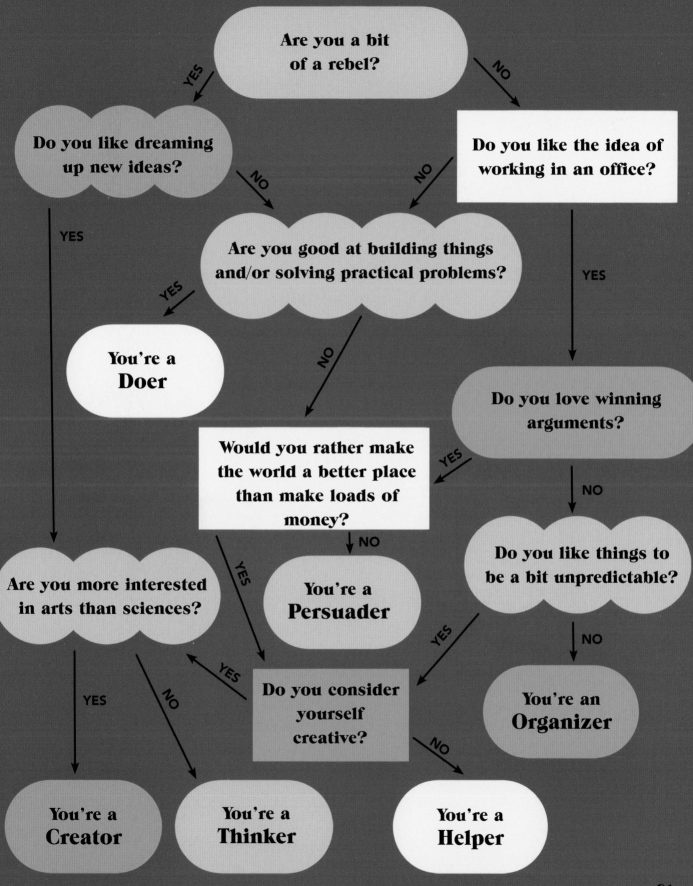

Are you a bit of a rebel?

YES

Do you like dreaming up new ideas?

NO

Do you like the idea of working in an office?

NO

Are you good at building things and/or solving practical problems?

YES

YES

You're a **Doer**

YES

Do you love winning arguments?

NO

Would you rather make the world a better place than make loads of money?

YES

Do you like things to be a bit unpredictable?

NO

You're a **Persuader**

YES

YES

Are you more interested in arts than sciences?

YES

Do you consider yourself creative?

NO

You're an **Organizer**

YES

NO

NO

You're a **Creator**

You're a **Thinker**

You're a **Helper**

Answers

Ready to find your dream job? Check out your "type" and see how well you think it matches up with your personality and interests...

Obviously, this quiz divides people and jobs up pretty simply, and in reality things are much more complex, but hopefully it will give you a helpful idea of the kind of job you might enjoy.

Doer

Doers are practical and realistic, with a knack for solving tricky problems on the spot. They like to keep learning new skills and improving their technical or specialist knowledge, in order to put it into action out in the world. They love building and fixing things, and being able to see the results of their hard work.

Doer jobs: Firefighter, builder, pilot, plumber, gardener, car mechanic

Thinker

Thinkers love to thoroughly investigate a subject, learning as much as they can and trying to see everything from different angles in order to truly understand it better. They enjoy working on complex ideas, and can spend a long time absorbed in something without getting bored.

Thinker jobs: Scientist, academic, engineer, investigative journalist, researcher

Persuader

Persuaders are great at talking people around to what they want them to believe, so are often good at making sales and winning arguments. They are often drawn to money and power, and enjoy the thrill of beating the competition and getting ahead.

Persuader jobs: Real estate agent, lawyer, business owner, public relations officer

Creator

Creators are artistic, original thinkers who are happiest when they're being creative in one or many different ways. They often prefer to make up their own rules and routine, being freer to explore new creative ideas and going with the flow when inspiration strikes.

Creator jobs: Musician, graphic designer, artist, writer, photographer

Helper

Helpers are responsible, caring people who want to make life better for others and love taking an active role in bringing about positive change. They are often sociable, and like interacting with other people in their daily work.

Helper jobs: Teacher, doctor, social worker, nurse, vet, charity worker

Organizer

Organizers are the rule makers of the world. Reliable and detail-focused, they keep everyone in line and make sure things run smoothly. They often prefer working with data to dealing directly with people, who don't always respect proper rules and processes.

Organizer jobs: Accountant, insurance officer, computer programmer, office manager

Understanding the Unconscious

What exactly is the unconscious mind? Well, it really depends on who you're asking...

If you could travel a hundred years back in time and have a chat with Sigmund Freud, whose ideas had a huge influence on 20th-century psychology, he would describe a murky and mysterious inner world, full of wild urges and dark impulses that your conscious mind struggles—and often fails—to keep in check. But if you talked to a neuroscientist today, it would probably sound a lot less scary.

Scientists now typically think of the unconscious mind as the vast collection of thoughts and processes pinging around our brain without us being consciously aware of or in control of them. This unconscious activity can be really helpful, as we've seen in the creative thinking process (page 71), but it could also mean that negative or unhelpful thoughts can affect our behavior without us even realizing it. Eek!

Personality and the unconscious

Freud believed that our personality is defined by how we manage the conflict between the three parts of our mind: the Id, Ego, and Superego. He described the Id as our unconscious, primitive self, which cares only about satisfying its instinctive urges—it wants what it wants, and it wants it NOW. The Superego is what we think of as our conscience, the little voice telling us how we should behave in a morally right way. And the Ego is the mostly conscious peacekeeper that tries to control the powerful Id, and get it what it wants in a way that feels more acceptable.

A lot of Freud's theories have been challenged and dismissed over the years, but this key idea—that we don't have total awareness of or control over the way we think and behave—was groundbreaking in his day, and seems to hold up pretty well even now.

Let's think about a real-life example—have you ever lost your temper at someone over a little thing, and realized later on that you'd actually been angry about something completely different and just taken it out on them? If so, you're not alone. Our unconscious thoughts, feelings, and impulses can be more powerful than we realize, and the way we manage them can affect how people—including ourselves—experience our personality.

Testing the unconscious

The unconscious mind is a huge, complex, and mysterious subject, but ways of testing how it works are often surprisingly simple. Rather than using true-or-false or yes-or-no questions or offering a set of multiple-choice options, tests for the unconscious tend to be "projective"—that is, they ask someone to respond to vague, open questions and prompts. The idea is that this type of test allows the mind to wander and express itself more freely, revealing the raw, instinctive workings of the unconscious mind.

For example, maybe you've heard of the Rorschach test? The idea is that people will see different things in a random inkblot shape, depending on the contents and concerns of their unconscious mind. Try this one.

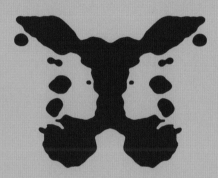

Some psychologists, particularly in the past, interpreted the answers people gave to projective tests very strictly, with set ideas about what certain features in a drawing or particular words said about someone's personality. But many now criticize this approach as unscientific—how can they prove that their scoring system is valid, and not just something they made up that sort of sounds right?

That's not to say that projective tests are a waste of time, though. They are still used to help people start thinking more deeply about the way they see things, and unpicking the unconscious assumptions that lie beneath these views. Rather than trying to explain someone's entire personality on the basis of their answers, the person giving the test might instead use these answers as a jumping-off point to ask some more specific questions.

Projective Test

It's time for a different type of test altogether now, one that dives deep into your unconscious mind to bring all sorts of interesting things up to the surface...

In this three-part projective test, there are no right answers—it's completely personal, and impossible to pass or fail. In fact, the less you think about your answers before giving them, the better—go with your first instinct, rather than an answer you think you should give.

Are you ready to get to know parts of your personality that you never even knew existed? Let's get started…

Note: We all have thoughts, feelings, and memories that aren't so nice. This test is designed to be fun rather than serious, but thinking about yourself and the way you see the world can sometimes bring up feelings you might not expect. The best idea is to take this test with an adult you trust nearby, or sitting with you so you can talk with them if any tricky feelings come up for you.

What's going on here?

What's going on in this picture? Don't think; just write down your first thoughts right now.

You can add some more detail by thinking about these questions, if you haven't included answers to them in your initial thoughts.:

- What's the background story, the actions that have led up to this moment?
- What exactly is happening at this moment?
- What thoughts and feelings are these people having? Are they expressing them, or keeping them hidden?
- What will happen after the moment shown here? How will things end up for these characters?

Try asking a friend or a family member to try this test, too, so you can compare answers—it can be really interesting.

Quick draw!

Make sure you're paying really close attention now, because this test isn't like the last one—it involves some pretty complicated instructions. Okay, are you really concentrating? Really really? All right…

Draw a scientist.

Yep, that's it!

Don't spend any time thinking before you start drawing, try to finish quickly, and don't keep erasing it and starting again. The point isn't for the drawing to be perfect or absolutely true to life; it's just your attempt to show the picture in your head of what a scientist looks like.

Word association

You may have played word association games before and not thought anything of it, but Carl Jung—a very famous figure in the history of psychology—studied how the instinctive connections we make between words might reveal interesting things about our unconscious mind.

What's the first word you think of when you read the list of words below? It's best to write them down as quickly as you can—no thinking about it first. Don't worry about spelling or handwriting, either.

Even if your first thought seems strange, go with it—don't feel like you have to pick something that makes sense! Our minds can make all sorts of unexpected connections, and that's not a bad thing. Imagine how boring it would be if we all thought the exact same way.

Try comparing your answers to other people's to see how similar or different your word associations are. No peeking at each other's answers while you're taking the test, though.

paint	free
tree	city
tiger	window
clever	good
sun	sea

Answers

If you're here looking for your score on this test, I've got some bad news...this time, there aren't any scores, categories, or measurements. Instead, it's up to you to think about your answers and what they might reveal about your unconscious thoughts, feelings, and ways of responding to the world around you.

Ready to explore the hidden depths of your unconscious? Here are some pointers to help guide your journey of self-discovery...

What's going on here?

The idea of this test is that people can often have very different ideas about what's going on in the picture, because they're projecting their own experiences, thoughts, and worries onto the characters. For example, do you think either of the two people in the picture look nervous about swimming?

It can be really interesting to discuss your ideas with another person who has taken the test—you might be surprised to find out how different theirs are from yours.

Quick draw!

This test might seem ridiculously simple, but often what we draw "off the top of our head" reveals a lot about how we see the world. It can show us what we unconsciously believe to be the "normal" version of something, which often matches up with the stereotype that exists in our society.

David Wade Chambers first developed the Draw-a-Scientist Test around thirty-five years ago. He analyzed children's drawings for certain stereotypical details, such as whether the scientist was male and wearing a lab coat and glasses. He found that some children began imagining scientists in this way from a very young age, and more and more children did as they got older.

Look at your drawing and think about these questions:

Is your scientist male?
What color is their skin?
How old are they?
Are they wearing glasses?

Are they wearing a lab coat?
Do they have any piercings or tattoos?
Are they using a wheelchair or any other disability aid?

The stereotype of a scientist in Western society is still often a white man in glasses and a lab coat—and even though we know that in reality scientists look all sorts of ways, we can often still unconsciously absorb this stereotype and draw it in the test!

It's a good idea sometimes to take a moment to examine the unconscious ideas that shape the way we think and feel. Some of them may be unfair or unhelpful, and by being more aware of them we can try to consciously correct ourselves. For example, if you drew a scientist as a white man, you could try learning more about scientists who don't fit that description—over time, this should sink in and help change your unconscious impressions.

Word association

This test can be really interesting in the way that it suggests what your personal, unconscious ideas about certain objects and concepts might be. For example, if the sea makes you nervous you might have written down a negative word, such as "scary" or "dangerous," next to it.

What does "free" mean to you? Or "good"? Take some time to think about what you've written. If you've taken the test with other people, talk over the similarities and differences in your answers.

Glossary

anxiety   When people worry so much about one particular thing, or lots of different things, that it affects their health and what they feel they can do in life.

conscious   Describes thoughts, feelings, and other brain processes that you're aware of and have some degree of control over.

crystallized intelligence   A form of intelligence based on a person's ability to use the knowledge, experience, and skills that they've gained over their lifetime.

Ego   Nowadays, we tend to use "ego" to mean a person's sense of being important and worthy—often, not in a very flattering way. But Sigmund Freud, a very influential thinker in psychology, described the Ego (with a capital "e") more specifically as the mostly conscious peacekeeper that tries to control the powerful Id and get it what it wants in a way that feels more acceptable to the moralizing Superego.

empathy   The ability to put yourself in someone else's shoes and understand what they are feeling.

extrovert   According to most psychologists today, extroversion (being an extrovert) is a personality trait describing someone outgoing and excitable, who enjoys going out and spending time in groups. But many psychologists in the past, such as Carl Jung, thought this trait was so important that it was actually a personality type in itself. Jung thought the main difference between people was whether they were an extrovert or an introvert.

fluid intelligence   A form of intelligence based on a person's ability to reason and solve problems by identifying patterns and thinking logically, without any particular knowledge or past experience of the problem in hand.

genes   Tiny structures inside your body's cells that are made up of DNA, and that carry information about your features that were passed on from your parents—for instance, what color eyes you have.

humors   Four liquids—blood, phlegm, yellow bile, and black bile (eww)—that the ancient Greeks, and many people after them, thought existed in differing amounts in each person's body. They believed that having lots of one liquid made your personality a certain way—for example, people with excessive black bile were kind of brooding and emo.

Id   According to Sigmund Freud, a very influential thinker in psychology, this is our unconscious, primitive self. It only cares about satisfying its instinctive urges and impulses, and it's very impatient. Kind of like a toddler who throws a tantrum if they don't get ice cream RIGHT NOW.

impulsiveness   Describes when a person tends to act without really thinking beforehand. For example, an impulsive person might jump straight over a wall to fetch a ball without knowing how far the drop on the other side is. (P.S. Don't do that. Not smart.)

Intelligence Quotient (IQ) Test   The best-known test for measuring intelligence, based on answering questions to test different reasoning skills. It gives you a score based on how many questions you answer correctly and how advanced that is for your age, but many people now don't think it's very accurate. It may also discriminate based on someone's cultural background and other factors.

introvert   Most psychologists today talk about introversion (being an introvert) as a personality trait, describing someone who likes spending time alone and in quiet situations, and who can be quite sensitive and get overwhelmed. In the past, however, many psychologists—such as Carl Jung—thought of it as a personality type in itself and divided the world into either introverts or extroverts.

neophilia   Describes when a person loves new things and experiences, finding them exciting and fulfilling. For example, a neophile would probably want to hang out at new places rather than always doing the same thing.

neophobia Describes when a person dislikes or is fearful of new things and experiences, finding them uncomfortable or even threatening. A neophobe would probably much rather hang out in the same place with the same people, not risk trying something different.

neuron A specialized cell designed to pass information around the body. We have billions of them in our brain, zipping messages back and forth to each other. Thoughts, feelings, whatever you need—they're hard workers.

neuroscientist A person whose job it is to study the brain and nervous system.

personality trait The most common way for psychologists to approach personality studies nowadays is by thinking about which traits—collections of related habits, tendencies, and ways of thinking—we each have. For example, one of the "Big Five" traits in the Five Factor Model is Conscientiousness. The idea is that a person who scores highly as Conscientious is likely to be punctual, organized, hardworking, tidy, dependable, self-disciplined, and careful.

personality type A defined "way to be a person," made up of personality traits (see above) that are thought to group together. The idea is that people who share a certain personality type will think and act similarly, and in a notably different way from people with other personality types.

phrenology A pseudoscience (something that appears scientific, but isn't at all) based on feeling natural lumps and dents in people's skulls. The idea is that they correspond to certain personality traits—but they don't. Phrenology was popular around 200 years ago, but has been proven so wrong that hardly anyone believes in it today.

pop psychology Short for "popular psychology," this describes fun, light psychology content—like silly "What kind of chocolate bar would you be?" online quizzes—rather than anything based on serious scientific studies.

projective test A type of test that is based on open-ended questions and vague prompts, aiming to draw out your unconscious thoughts and feelings. Instead of true-or-false questions, for example, it might ask you to draw a tree. Easy, sure, but who knows what it will reveal about you…

psychologist A person whose job it is to study psychology, the science of the human mind, and try to figure out why people behave the way they do. They may work with patients, talking to them and trying to help them with mental health issues or other personal difficulties connected to their patterns of thinking and feeling.

researcher A person whose job it is to carry out scientific or other kinds of research, discovering or further exploring information about a particular topic.

Superego A term used by Sigmund Freud, a very influential thinker in psychology, to describe what we often think of as our conscience—the little voice telling us how we should behave in a morally right way.

Unconscious Today, we mostly use this term to describe anything that we do without being fully aware of it. For instance, scientists studying the brain can see that there are lots of processes going on in there that we're not aware of at all. However, for famed psychology thinker Sigmund Freud, the Unconscious (capital "u") is our murky and mysterious inner world—full of wild urges and dark impulses that our conscious mind struggles—and often fails—to keep in check.

zodiac signs Twelve signs representing different areas of the sky, and linked to different dates in the year. They're also known as star signs, and they're a key feature of astrology, a popular but unscientific way of thinking about how stars and other objects moving through space affect human lives.

Index

So You Want to Be a Psychologist?

If you think that a career in psychology might be just right for you, you're in luck. There are all sorts of psychologist jobs to choose from. Here are just a few to get you thinking…

Sport and exercise psychologist

Are you a total sports fiend? A good listener who enjoys offering people practical solutions? Do you like to help others reach their full potential? Then ready-set-GO get that sport and exercise psychologist job.

Sport and exercise psychologists can work with all sorts of clients: world-famous football teams, first-time marathon runners, swimming coaches, cricket umpires, e-sports players—anyone at all, as long as they care enough about their performance to hire you.

A good sport and exercise psychologist needs to be good at understanding people's needs and capable of conjuring up bags of positive energy to help motivate them when they might just feel like giving up. Being a sports fan is pretty important, too.

Clinical psychologist

Are you interested in helping people who are facing issues such as anxiety, depression, and eating disorders? Do you like the idea of studying complex subjects and applying your knowledge to real-life situations? Then you might enjoy working as a clinical psychologist.

Clinical psychologists can have many roles, including assessing people's needs with tests and interviews, teaming up with other health professionals to develop treatment programs, carrying out research to further our scientific knowledge, and providing expert advice to people in other fields—such as law or business.

Working as a clinical psychologist can be challenging, as you may be in contact with many different people who are very distressed. It can also be quite competitive, but don't let that stop you. If your ideal job combines science with caring for people, it might suit you perfectly.

Forensic psychologist

Are you fascinated by crime, and what makes people commit it? Have you got a will of steel to get the job done even when things get really tough? Do you want to help give people a second chance and make the world a safer place? Then a career in forensic psychology might be right up your alley.

As a forensic psychologist, you will likely work in a range of locations—including prisons, secure hospitals, and police stations—in noisy, hectic, or time-pressured conditions. You may be carrying out individual assessments, developing rehabilitation programs, or shaping policies to better help offenders and victims.

A high level of empathy is very important in this job, as the goal is to help people rather than judge and punish them. However, the role could be very challenging if you tend to take things very personally or find it hard to cope with strong emotions, as you may often work with people who don't want your help or whose circumstances make you very sad or angry.

Psychotherapist

Do you like having deep conversations about hopes, feelings, and fears? Are you the friend that everyone turns to if they're having problems? Do you think you could stay strong and calm when trying to help people who are really sad, confused, or scared? Then you might suit working as a psychotherapist.

Psychotherapists aim to help clients understand and manage problems such as mental health issues, painful emotions, and difficult habits, thoughts, or behaviors. Most therapies are based on talking, but you can specialize in different types of therapy, such as art, dance, or drama therapies, which use these activities to help people express themselves and work through their issues.

It can be tough to work with people experiencing really difficult times, so it's important to look after yourself and make sure you have lots of support. If you love to care for others but aren't so good at accepting help yourself, try to work on that. You'll be preparing yourself really well for this role—and life in general.

So You Want to Know More About Psychology?

If you want to find out more about psychology and get a taste of what it's like
to work as a psychologist, here are a few good books and online videos to start with…

Books

Looking After Your Mental Health
by Alice James and Louie Stowell (Usborne)

People often find it a lot easier to talk about their physical health than their mental health, but it's just as important to get help with worries and difficult feelings as it is to see a doctor for your various aches and pains. This book will help you better understand what good mental health feels like, and guide you through situations that might cause strong emotions.

Mind Your Head
by Juno Dawson and Dr. Olivia Hewitt (Hot Key Books)

We need to take good care of our mind—it's the only one we've got. This funny, fact-packed book looks at all sorts of topics related to mental health, from anxiety and depression to personality disorders and addictive behaviors. It includes real-life stories from a range of young people facing different issues, and gives advice on how to manage different challenging situations. Clinical psychologist Dr. Olivia Hewitt, one of the book's authors, gives lots of expert information and support from her professional perspective.

Videos

The Psych Show with Dr. Ali Mattu: How Do Psychologists Analyze People?
youtube.com/watch?v=_oQGCOe7Vvc

This short video by clinical psychologist Dr. Ali Mattu addresses the popular myth that psychologists can't help analyzing everyone they meet. Learn more about what is and isn't ethical psychologist behavior, and why diagnosing celebrities' mental states based on how they appear to be acting is always a bad idea…

CrashCourse Psychology: Psychological Research
youtube.com/watch?v=hFV71QPvX2I

Psychological research is key to helping us understand the human mind, separating our hunches, myths, and assumptions from the scientific reality of how people actually think and behave. This video gives an introduction to the what, how, and why of psychological research, explaining important terms such as "control group," "random sample," and "double-blind procedure." It explores what good and bad research might look like, and how psychologists come to wrong or misleading conclusions if they don't do things the right way.

Red Bull Gaming: The Role of Sports Psychology in Esports
youtube.com/watch?v=8PsvE1G6_GM

If you're more interested in playing games on a computer screen than a sports field, then don't assume sports psychology isn't the career for you. Sports psychologist Mia Stellberg works with top e-sports teams, helping to improve their performance by focusing on players' well-being and ability to cope with stress and strong emotions. This video gives an idea of what sports psychology looks like in the ever-growing area of competitive gaming, and how Stellberg gets results by encouraging players to build up their self-esteem and live a more balanced life.

Inspiring | Educating | Creating | Entertaining

Brimming with creative inspiration, how-to projects, and useful information to enrich your everyday life, Quarto Knows is a favorite destination for those pursuing their interests and passions. Visit our site and dig deeper with our books into your area of interest: Quarto Creates, Quarto Cooks, Quarto Homes, Quarto Lives, Quarto Drives, Quarto Explores, Quarto Gifts, or Quarto Kids.

First published in 2020 by Wide Eyed Editions, an imprint of The Quarto Group.
100 Cummings Center, Suite 265D, Beverly, MA 01915, USA.
T +1 978-282-9590 F +1 078-283-2742 **www.QuartoKnows.com**

A CIP record for this book is available from the Library of Congress.

ISBN 978-0-7112-6674-2

The illustrations were created digitally.
Set in Avenir and Grouch

Published by Georgia Amson-Bradshaw
Designed by Myrto Dimitrakoulia
Edited by Lucy Brownridge
Production by Dawn Cameron

Manufactured in Guangdong, China TT022021

9 8 7 6 5 4 3 2 1